C000119062

Fragments:

Essays and Philosophies

Elizabeth A. Ward

Black Typewriter Publications

The author is grateful for the use of excerpts from the following copyrighted material:

Aphramor, L. and Bacon, L. (2014) *Body Respect: What Conventional Health Books Get Wrong, Leave Out, and Just Plain Fail To Understand About Weight.* Dallas, TX, BenBella Books.

Baker, Jes (2018) *Landwhale: Why Insults Are Just Really Cute Nicknames, Body Image Is Hard, and Diets Can Kiss My Ass.* Berkeley, CA, Seal Press.

Krznaric, R (2014) *Empathy: A Handbook For Revolution.* London, Rider Books.

Haig, M (2018) *Notes On A Nervous Planet.* Edinburgh, Canongate.

Cain, S (2013) *Quiet: The Power of Introverts In A World That Can't Stop Talking.* London, Penguin.

Helgoe, L (2013) *Introvert Power: Why Your Inner Life Is Your Hidden Strength.* Naperville, Ill, Sourcebooks.

Brown, B (2013) *Daring Greatly: How The Courage To Be Vulnerable Transforms The Way We Live, Love, Parent and Lead.* London, Portfolio Penguin.

De Beauvoir, S (1947) *The Second Sex.* London, Vintage.

Thomas, I (2011) *I Wrote This For You.* Central Avenue Publishing.

ISBN: 978-1-9993228-0-9

Published by Black Typewriter Publications
http://catsandchocolate.com

Dedication

For Marjorie and Mary, dedicated book lovers, you are missed.
To all those who feel like outsiders—take heart, the world needs
you.

Contents

Introduction: Assembling The Jigsaw

This book is all about what it means to live, think, feel, and love in the twenty-first century. It came about from a suggestion by my sister to write a book of essays; at the time, I was struggling with my novel writing. I already write essays. In fact, I've written more essays than any other type of writing. This is because I've been a blogger for at least twelve years, writing personal essays, opinion pieces, reviews, and poetry. In-between I've done two degrees, both of which involved intensive essay writing. My work as an arts and culture journalist means that writing essays and non-fiction are at the forefront of my creative life.

I'd describe what I do now, on the blog in particular, as a cross between opinion, life writing, and philosophising. I try to be authentic and true to myself, which is what I feel all deeply meaningful writing should aim towards, in order to develop a writing voice. I always try my hardest to aim for inspiring, informing, and having a dialogue with people about what it means to live in this world of ours. I believe that creative expression is essential for our sanity in a world that seems increasingly uncertain and often downright scary. I don't just mean writing, art, and culture, but I also mean creative in terms of making and living—food, problem solving, going on adventures, social interactions. I feel that connecting with people is the most essential thing we can do in a time where loneliness and alienation is commonplace.

My writing, and my blogging, is simply the way that I bridge those two concepts. By writing, I am thinking up solutions, sharing, creating, describing experiences, and asking questions. Writing is the way that I connect with people. I want readers to ask questions of their own, to seek out their own answers, to share their own thoughts, memories, and feelings. This book is my offering to people—my thoughts and my feelings—on topics that have arisen in the past thirty years of my life. Not everything will be something you can relate to. They are conduits for you to think about your own life, and your own experiences.

Why did I decide to call this book 'Fragments'? It's because these essays are fragments that make up a part of a whole. They are broken glass, slips of thought and identity. Identity is a slippery thing— some things remain the same, but we are always changing with time and our experiences. Identity has fascinated me since I was a teenager—first, with all the things I collected around me as signifiers of 'me', and most recently with identity politics—what it means to be a woman, to be deaf, and in my generation, to live in a body. I am still only fragments, with pieces of myself appearing in different situations. In this way, writing is a way of looking for that core of self, of trying to recognise it—and yet learning that perhaps, I will never truly know. Identity is both something we can see, and something invisible.

In this way, I begin by writing about the body. I'm a white cisgender (where birth sex and gender identity match) profoundly deaf woman, and have also experienced most of my life on the larger side of the body spectrum. I have spent much of my bodily experience veering between a lack of self-confidence, and learning to accept and love my body. Body-acceptance and self-love are always a daily work in progress, even though my aim is to always move towards radical body positivity and liberation. Here, I want to challenge perceptions of what 'acceptable' and 'normal' mean, and to ask questions about the body and identity. The way we experience our bodies has a lot to do with how we see the world, and how we move within it. My experience of the world in this body of mine may be different to how you experience the world through your body, and that is both interesting and should be celebrated.

Next, I move on to writing about the realm of the heart—relationships and emotion. Here, I am writing about love, emotions, connection. To write about relationships and emotions is a way of solidifying what matters in life—the lasting things, that keep our hearts open and keep us grounded, and grateful. I'm not someone who believes that thinking deeply means turning off emotions. Emotions are what make us human, whether or not we use them to guide us. They have a major effect on how we express ourselves, and how we relate to other people. Emotions come alive when we are experiencing the world, when we are watching a film, reading a book, or listening to music. The way we feel about people, animals, ourselves, and the world around us is something worth exploring. Life is profoundly more beautiful because of the people we know, and the connections we make (or not, as might be the case).

In 'Thinking and Dreaming', I explore the different aspects of what it means to be a thinking, sentient being, with all the joys and difficulties connected to it. In this section, you will find me writing about introversion, laziness, depression, imagination, and purpose. These essays are about considering what part the mind, psychology, and thought plays in life and identity. The subjects I write about here are thought-experiments, a celebration of thinking and the brain. I connect my own experiences with what I've read, and what I've seen, and used them to come up with solutions or questions. Sometimes, those questions go unanswered—not all questions in life have one definitive answer that fits us all. I write about surfacing from depression, and the battle of will and feeling that it takes to come to life again. I have written a letter for the dreamers amongst us—to reassure and inspire.

The fourth section of the book is about writing and creativity. On first look, it may seem like the odd section out—as if it doesn't quite belong—but for me, writing, reading, and creativity is an intrinsic part of the fragmented puzzle that makes up my life and identity. It is true that we are not what we do—we may be workers, writers, artists, professionals—but occasionally, what we do does affect the way we see the world, and what interests us. Writing is what I do and not what I am—and yet I would not be who I am without expressing myself through writing. In the same way that being an introvert affects how I interact with people, and how I experience the world, writing allows me to refract my experiences and what I imagine, and put them somewhere. What I write is not me—it goes out into the world and the people reading my words interpret them how they will, with their own experiences and imagination—but at one point, these words came from whatever part of myself felt that need to express something. I explore how to keep yourself motivated, how to use your energy, the writers that I love and am inspired by, and my experience of being a blogger, amongst essays about the subjects that most interest me. If you're a budding writer or artist, or have always wanted to begin, or add more creativity to your life, I hope something here sparks your journey.

In the final section, 'Society and Identity', we come full circle. Throughout the last twenty years of writing, I've explored deaf identity and deaf issues in different mediums—blogging, poems, articles—and yet my deaf identity is still contentious, something that isn't fixed. In the essay *Sound Memories*, I try to write a short autobiography of deafness, of my journey thus far. Then later on, the essay *Deaf Identities* is an attempt to explore the various deaf identities that are possible, and yet still end up with a sense of ambiguity, of floating somewhere in the middle. Is it important to try to define ourselves with labels that might no longer truly fit? Does it matter whether or not we 'belong' to particular communities, when we can find our own sense of belonging within ourselves and amongst friends?

The essay *Girl, Woman, Feminine, Feminist* is an exploration of girlhood and womanhood, and how I have arrived at feminism. It's not extraordinary that I have found my way towards identifying as a feminist, because women and girls often do, considering the inequalities and small (and large) acts of sexism we are faced with. In these uncertain times, where the rights of women and girls are constantly eroded, a discussion of feminism is more essential than ever.

In this section, too, I discuss aspects of society that I feel are broken, and difficult to understand. That perhaps our only way forward is to keep an open mind and heart, and be compassionate— to others and ourselves. What do I feel will make the most difference in the coming years ahead, when we are likely to see and hear news that disturbs us, that will change our lives and test us to the breaking point? Where do we go for solace and comfort, and what can we do when the world looks as if it is falling apart? How can we fight for each other, for a brighter future? Nobody can do such a big undertaking alone, and it will be community and coming together that will make all the difference. What does a better world look like? I try to describe what I believe in, and how that translates to action.

In all of this, my underlying state is hope and optimism. Much of the time, I struggle with negativity, overcome with the many problems encountered each day and within wider society. Yet, there are things that are worth fighting for, more than worth living for, and this book is an attempt to explore some of those subjects. Every one of the people reading this book will be different and take different impressions away with them. My hope is that my thoughts give you, in turn, optimism and a sense of courage.

Part One:

Living in a Body

To My Body: A Letter

You carry me through the world, one step after another, sometimes painfully, sometimes joyfully, but always forwards. We've been through a lot together, and there are times I have wished you different. There are times that I have longed to be uncaged and to fly across the world, having nothing to weigh myself down, nothing to pull me down and remind me of my mortality, my finite time, on this strange and wondrous place we call earth.

You have scars. We have weathered those scars together. I know that parts of you are somehow slightly broken: in need of more care than a body without these issues will need. I know that I have wished that we took up less space, yet I am joyful that we can take up that space too. We take up space and there is more of me for other people and myself. Of course, it hasn't been easy for you. I struggle daily with two opposing ideas: that I am enough, that my body is a gift, and yet that this body I have is not socially acceptable. Each day I reach towards a place where I can embrace all that you are.

You can do so much. You can dance, feel a rhythm and absorb it and move within it. You can stretch towards the sky, opening arms wide and embracing the air. Your hands press computer keys and words appear on the screen. You can swim—push through the water in strong strokes, buoyed and powerful. I am frequently startled by how much I can lift, how much power your arms and legs have. My face can express sorrow in the lines across the forehead, spirit can leak out in the light of a smile, and my voice, though quiet, tries to express the swirl of thoughts firing through the brain's network of neurons. Your steps can be both heavy and light. I can sprint like the wind when I need to. I won't be running a marathon any time soon, but sometimes it feels good to have the wind in my hair.

You can feel other people's moods: sometimes for good, sometimes for bad. At times I feel like I am losing my grasp on reality—feeling the vibes and energy other people release—and I wonder if what I am feeling is mine or theirs. Too much of other people's pain can eat away at the spirit. Yet I wouldn't magic it away. There are many lessons to be learnt from feeling and understanding other people's pain, as well as your own. I hold pain in the gut, and in the chest, and have learnt to release it with the breath. It's a work in progress, but I believe that with time, I will be wiser for it. To move through the world is to feel and suffer. To move through those feelings and understand them is one of the best lessons I can learn. I believe that there are other senses that we haven't named, that aren't part of common understanding: senses that we tap into without quite realising it. Intuition, reading energy and body language, 'knowing' things without knowing how.

I love that I can smell something and be transported into a memory. My sense of smell is one of the strongest senses, followed by sight and taste. The human sense of smell has become blunted over time, but just as people see differently, they can experience scents differently. How incredible is it that people can compensate so much for a sense that other people might consider a tragedy to not fully experience? And how wonderful is it that this brain can remember sounds I no longer hear and recognise them when I wear my aids? It's a complicated thing, to understand the relationship I have with hearing. It's bound up with memory and identity, and above all, acceptance. I may fear that I will lose more of it, but I live each day grateful for what I have, too. I am always learning from the people around me what it means to move in this world as someone who is deaf. You are resilient, and have weathered these storms of uncertainty. I know that there may be more storms to come in the future, but with this body, I will survive them—perhaps a little battered and shaken, but with bravery.

Perhaps this is also a good time to apologise. For those times I have accused you of ugliness, looking in the mirror and turning away, and feeling that you are not good enough. The shame that comes with social expectations. I have been deeply unkind to you, and have not appreciated what I do have. Yet I am trying hard every day to see what is beautiful, what is miraculous, and what enables me to do what I love to do—my hands, my feet, my heart, and my eyes— to do and see and experience the world in this particular vessel. Nobody has the same DNA, the same genetic makeup. We are all unique, all different, yet so similar. I feel the injustice of it, the unkindness I have showed you, a chasm and swirl of criticism directed towards you, and I am so very sorry. Imagine all the years wasted feeling this way, self-consciously afraid of other people's perceptions, of the way I have internalised the messages I picked up from the world around me. You are enough. You are incredible. You keep me breathing and moving, and seeing, and touching and feeling, and thinking.

Let me talk about the future, the one in which you and I will experience, feel, think, and see new things. Time is always hard on human bodies, but I like to think that each new wrinkle is a mark of wisdom. Each new line around the mouth is a memory of joy. No matter how many strange events occur in the galaxy of this body, I always hope for the best. There may be new pains, new challenges, and difficult experiences we will have to face together. So long as I remember how very amazing you are, to have brought me this far, I feel that we will always weather those tumultuous storms together. We will keep dancing, and smiling, and giving and receiving, thinking bland and interesting thoughts, and being both silly and profound. It's a strange and humbling life, to live in a body, but one that will always be worth the challenge.

Hair

Most of us have hair. Some have little, some have masses of it. It grows on skin, on our scalp, places we'll never see. It can be fine, invisibly golden, or dark and coarse. For male-identified people, hair is not so much of a cultural issue. You shave it, or don't. You have a lot of it, or don't. Nobody bats an eyelid at men's hairy legs (or even their smooth legs, if that's your thing), dark arm hair, their beards or moustaches. Even the hairiest amongst men isn't out of the ordinary.

I have been secretly doing battle with the hair on my body since I was made aware that I have more hair, supposedly, than most women have. On my chest, on my face, even on my legs and arms. I was diagnosed with PCOS in my teens, and apart from the hormone imbalances and insulin resistance, it means an excess of androgens and testosterone. My hair and I have been on a long and difficult journey together.

A side note here: I would never presume to tell anyone what to do with their own body hair. Body hair modification used to be a hot topic within feminist discussions, particularly when someone first came to awareness of feminism. It was mostly about criticism of the pressures that women-identified people came under to remove the hair on their bodies to be considered attractive, particularly to men, a way to perform femininity and 'smoothness'. You don't have to have hairy legs to be a feminist, and neither should you feel pressure to shave your legs if that isn't something you want to do. However, women-identified people often feel that cultural, social pressure to have hairless legs, particularly in summer if you have shorts or are wearing a dress—or even going swimming. In recent years, the discussion is more about examining our own ambiguous relationship to hair removal, the reasons behind them, and the environmental costs of these practices (such as the chemicals used in depilatory creams, disposal of razors and plastic, and so on). In a way, self-examination is less about controlling what other people do, and more about our own values and whether it is possible to adapt or change our actions to bring them more in line with our values.

As a teenager, long before I knew about the PCOS, the first inkling I had of how women and girls removed their hair was a classmate in the last year of primary school (fifth grade in the US) remarking that we would soon be able to remove our underarm hair, because we were nearly at the age we could. Like some of the girls in my class, at age 11 we were experiencing the beginnings of puberty, with hair, mood swings, and some of us our first periods.

My family wasn't the kind that worried so much about hair-removal or unnecessary modification of the body, so it wasn't until then that I considered what this meant. I felt betrayed by my own body: something that was meant to be private was all too public, seeing as somehow, the entire class found out that I had started my period. My changing body wasn't something to be explored in my own way, but in a humiliating, self-conscious way. Eventually, though, I found ways to deal with it, learning not to care what other people thought.

The first time I had a sports day at secondary school (sixth to twelfth grade in the US), I was told to wear shorts, despite my anxiety about how hairy my legs were. And they were hairy—dark, curly hair, at odds with the colour of the hair on my head, which was more of a mid-brown with lighter highlights. I hadn't yet started to shave or slather my legs in foul smelling depilatory cream. A friend made another comment—she sympathised, and said she also had trouble with hairy legs, despite how smooth they were. I tried not to let it get to me, but it became clearer that most girls I knew either hid their legs in tracksuit trousers or had hairless, depilated skin. My arms were also dark-haired, thicker than most of the girls and women I knew. Often within my own group of friends, we would discuss hair removal, reiterating how shameful it was to have visible hair—discussing threading, waxing, and sugaring. In women's magazines, 'beauty is pain' was a mantra, and more than once another girl said this to me, a kind of strange, masochistic compliment when we were talking about how we plucked our eyebrows.

So I began depilating and shaving my legs. Most often when I knew I was having PE or going swimming, even just because. I liked their smoothness, I felt more feminine—but it was a pain. I tried waxing, the resulting small, painful bumps on my skin, the burning on my legs, putting me off ever doing it again. I didn't touch the hair on my arms, feeling that if I did that, I could never go back—I didn't feel like dealing with shaving rashes on my arms or the scratchy, coarse regrowth. Of course I knew girls who shaved and waxed their arms, and part of me recoiled from the idea, even as young and uncritical as I was of 'beauty' culture. So I stuck to underarm and leg hair removal, through most of my teenage years—though less often in winter, when I barely removed my tights.

One of my doctors noticed that I had an 'excessive' amount of hair on my chest area. By excessive, she meant that it was dark and noticeable, so she recommended I be tested for PCOS (Polycystic Ovarian Syndrome), just in case. At this point I was already bleaching my fine dark moustache, and had a number of dark hairs on my neck. It felt both frustrating, miserable, and a relief that I had a reason for the darker hair I had on my body, but I entered a long period of battle with this hair that made me feel unfeminine, depressed, and unattractive. It was a couple of years before I discovered feminism, so I had no real safety net or critical analysis of why I felt so bad about having hair. At the time, I felt, again, betrayed by my body.

The hair on my face became darker and thicker. So I used crème bleach, depilatory cream designed for the face, tweezers, scissors. Later on, I used an epilator designed for the face—which was time consuming and painstaking. With the epilator, I went through so many batteries, and I probably could have taken out shares in a number of hair removal companies, as another friend with PCOS once said. It felt like a never-ending battle, a sad balance between trying different courses of pills (notably Dianette and Yasmin, both of which were good for a while against the excess hormones, but made me depressed), different ways of removing hair, researching to find out if there was another, better way.

Until, finally, through a number of different ways, I found a balance between accepting myself as I was, and realising that I didn't want to spend my life constantly freaking out about hair. It's just hair. My current method is shaving, and though it's not ideal, it's cheap and works most days. I occasionally shave the hair on my chest, though most of the time I leave it be, figuring that most of my wardrobe doesn't expose it, and I'm more laid-back about hair these days anyway. I only shave my legs if I feel I want to. I'm not too worried about what other people think because they can take me as I am, and my body is mine, nobody else's. I do still occasionally feel unfeminine and there are days when the constant removal of the hair on my face makes me miserable, but self-acceptance is an ongoing, everyday thing, something always being worked on.

Why this shift? Feminism and a strong critique of the supposed 'beauty' rituals that women undertake had a lot to do with it. Examining my reasons for taking part in these practices, and realising the difference between doing something because it feels good, or makes you feel good, and doing something because you're afraid if you don't, people will see and treat you differently. The thing with feminism is that it's like having a pair of dark glasses peeled off your eyes that you didn't even know were there—this is why they call the awakening 'consciousness raising', because you see and understand that we are part of a patriarchal world culture that is bad for both women and men (and girls and boys, and all other genders). The idea that 'beauty is pain', or that we have to use up so much of our valuable time in the pursuit of an impossible ideal of the feminine is what keeps the so-called beauty industry rolling in money. They feed on our insecurities, inventing new 'problems' that can only be solved by using their products.

On the environmental and health front, when we consider the amount of chemicals used in production of 'beauty' products, lotions, and potions, it's difficult to understand why we still use some of them. Cream bleach contains hydrogen peroxide, depilatory creams contain chemicals that are strong enough to dissolve hair, and razors are not currently recycled easily, with disposable razors being the worst (plus plastic production is hazardous to the environment). We already come into contact with plenty of chemicals in our day to day lives, many of which have unknown effects on our body chemistry and DNA, so it is always worth trying to learn more about what we are using, how it affects our own bodies, and how it impacts the environment. There are still options that have less impact on our bodies and the environment, though it can be hard to find cost-effective solutions.

However, it's difficult when your relationship with cosmetics becomes complicated. If you truly do feel that you need products like concealer and foundation to feel good about yourself, or that if something like PCOS makes you feel less womanly (whatever that might mean), and using cosmetics gives a boost to your self-confidence, then maybe we shouldn't feel guilty about it. A relationship with cosmetics can be like an artist wielding tools, or a child with a box of paints—a way to exercise creativity. Both men and women, girls and boys, enjoy this kind of creativity, and it can be fun. I don't believe in shaming people for wearing make-up or engaging in beauty rituals. They have been around for millennia—just consider the Ancient Egyptians and their obsession with eyeliner and milk baths. Different cultures have different ideas of beauty, and pursue different kinds of rituals. Not that we can't critique those rituals, but that humans will always pursue adornments and body modification.

I used to spend a lot of money of cosmetics—not just hair removal cosmetics, but the whole gamut of products. To begin with, it was because I equated cosmetics with feeling good about myself, a way to practice self-care, and expressing myself. I liked, and still do like, the idea of luxurious pampering—taking some time out to spend an hour or two in the bathroom, having a bath, wearing a facemask, and painting my nails in a fun colour. And yet, with PCOS, a whole riot of symptoms meant that I became reliant on makeup when leaving the house. An activity that I enjoyed as fun became a chore—eruptions of spots needing concealer, oily skin needing liberal applications of powder.

Even gaining an understanding of my own relationship with the beauty industry and how I've opted-in to it, it remains a complicated subject that can't be separated from issues of self-esteem and confidence. In many ways, I am not fully 'there' yet, and even with all the tools I have at my disposal—body positivity, self-acceptance, feminism—some days are a struggle. Especially in a culture that still places enormous pressures on women and girl-identified people to look a certain way. I don't want women or girls (or men or boys) to feel bad about the way they look, or to feel they can't be accepted for themselves, warts and all. I feel accepted as I am by my family and close friends, and wouldn't dream of not accepting them as they are. My own self-acceptance is an ongoing thing, which varies from day to day, and something that requires constant work. Given that I can't see myself giving up dealing with my facial hair, or covering my spots with concealer (unless I'm not planning on going anywhere), this is an ongoing dialogue between my values, ideals, and the reality of my relationship with my own body.

In the end, hair is just hair, and if you accept that we are evolved from apes—many moons ago—and that we are warm-blooded mammals, it is unlikely to disappear any time soon. Whatever you do—keep it or not—is both a highly personal decision, and yet something that can be dictated by cultural pressures and norms. Ultimately, we get to decide what we want to do with our bodies, and if you're happy (like me) to keep the armpit and leg hair until summer arrives, I salute you. It takes a certain amount of courage in the face of disapproving social-norms to keep our bodies as they are, and to love ourselves warts, hair, and all.

Body Positive

In an ideal world, we would live in a society where all bodies are considered valid and beautiful. I believe that all bodies—fat, thin, short, tall, disabled, neuro-diverse, trans, and everything in between—are deserving of love and acceptance. For me, there are no qualifiers. There is no—all bodies are beautiful *but* it's important to be healthy. 'Healthy' looks different to everyone. 'Healthy' feels different for everyone. To me, this is not a discussion about health, but about the basic right for every person to feel as if they deserve to accept and love their body. And to be loved and accepted by those they are closest to. Our particularly white, Western, cultural ideas of beauty (both male and female) are deeply problematic. We live in a world that values the superficial and a particular narrow—white, cisgender, slim, toned and muscular (for men), photoshopped, heterosexual—image that we are conditioned to believe is desirable, or at least exposed to everywhere we look. We have corporations and the media pushing particular images towards us, regurgitating the same images over and over, packaged in different ways—until we believe there is something wrong with us because we don't fit (and can never fit) that mould.

Body positivity is a movement that aims to celebrate body diversity, to change the discussion around beauty and bodies, and to break the cycle of hate and self-hatred that pervades society. Naomi

Wolf's *The Beauty Myth*, was one of the first texts to go in-depth into a discussion of the harm that cultural ideas and ideals of 'beauty' do to women in particular. However, it is becoming increasingly common for men and boys to also feel inadequate and as if they have to attain a particular type of body to be loved and accepted, to be deemed attractive. At the heart of all this, is our very real need to be loved and accepted—to be seen, to feel good in our bodies, and to celebrate the body we have now, and everything that it can do. To liberate ourselves from the desire to engage in harmful practices, cultural values and outside expectations.

Girls as young as five are already becoming indoctrinated into diet culture. Imagine feeling that your body is wrong at that age. As Megan Jayne Crabbe says in her book, *Body Positive Power*, you just have to look at the statistics, from various sources and publications, to understand that many of us have been, or are, deeply unhappy with our bodies because we believe that we have to attain a particular thin, model-esque ideal. Only 5% of the population, mostly models and film stars, have the kind of 'ideal' look that we are told is something to aspire towards. Who tells us to aspire towards that look? It's impossible to not be affected by the images we see day in and day out—on billboards, in adverts, in films, in magazines and newspapers, anywhere you care to look. The women around us, even when we are a child, have an impact on how we see our own bodies. The behaviours and attitudes around us have a profound effect on our own self-image.

A great deal of conversations I've had over the years, and some of the conversations I've been there for, have shown me how disconnected we are from living in the bodies we have. I'm no stranger to body dissatisfaction, to feeling shame and struggling with comparison. I've had to come to terms with a body that has a metabolic syndrome, isn't as efficient as supposed 'normal' female bodies, and I've struggled with the way I look in comparison to women who I (perceive) don't have to worry about 'excessive' hair on their faces, chest, and arms. I've given up on many women's magazines that unhealthily mock women for their (normal, healthy) cellulite, for their weight gain or loss, and in the same breath tell us patronisingly how to accept ourselves and our bodies, whilst pushing the latest fad diet. I've opted out of comparison culture, and have tried to teach myself, by way of fat activism, HAES (health at every size), and the fatshion community, to love and accept myself without reservation.

Yet, every single day I live in this culture of the beauty myth and where I am surrounded by strong, beautiful women who have difficult, painful relationships with their bodies, and I know I am always a few steps away from self-loathing. Body love doesn't mean we are always going to love our bodies, but that we can at least accept them the way they are, and strive towards that liberation, the freedom, as Jes Baker puts it in her memoir, *Landwhale*, from 'all outside expectations, even our own. Liberation is not having to love your body all the time. Liberation is not asking permission to be included in society's ideal of beauty. Liberation is bucking the concept of beauty as currency altogether. Liberation is recognizing the systemic issues that surround us and acknowledging that perhaps we're not able to fix them all on our own. Liberation is personally giving ourselves permission to live life.'

Self-loathing is an epidemic. It might not seem like it in an age of selfies and fashion bloggers, but it truly is something that most of us struggle with in one way or another. Whether because of our exposure to social media, advertising, a culture that is founded upon colonial, patriarchal roots, and where capitalism convinces us that body love, beauty, and happiness can be bought, most of us may be struggling with some kind of deep seated issues around body image and self-love. Especially if you are outside of the supposed 'norm' of white, cisgender, sculpted, and unblemished. Most of us are outside of this, in different ways. The skin is generally not unblemished or always smooth, unmarked, or unwrinkled. Wrinkles are a sign that you smile and have laughed and cried, that you have lived. Most of the people I know are subject to spots or marks every now and then, some more often than others. People are as diverse as our DNA, and just as diverse in appearance. Wouldn't life be boring and strange if we all looked the same?

I believe that selfies can be important. I don't agree that it's a sign of vanity if someone takes 'selfies'. Self-portraiture is an important step towards accepting yourself and seeing your body as it is, getting used to what you look like from different angles, in different contexts, and at different ages. Some people find it incredibly hard to take or share self-portraits, myself included. There is an element of fear and shame when you allow yourself to be seen, or to see yourself. Yet the more often you do it, the more often you come to accept and even love yourself as you are.

Your relationship with yourself is an important one—only you live in your body, know exactly what you're feeling and thinking, and can be your own worst enemy or the most important friend you'll ever have. If you love or accept your body, then you are much more likely to treat it well, to feed yourself, to move yourself in the ways you like to move, to practice self-care when you need it most. Loving yourself, being as positive as you are able about the body you live in, and rejecting shame and comparison, is a sure-fire way of taking ownership of your own life and bodily autonomy.

The idea that we are narcissistic if we take self-portraits is a myth. Narcissism is the wrong word to use—narcissism in psychology is a disorder characterised as being unable to empathise with others, and an inflated sense of self-importance. It is a real disorder with various other symptoms and pathologies, and shouldn't be used lightly outside a medical context, unless you are sure they exhibit all the signs and behaviours of someone with narcissistic personality disorder. Narcissism as used in popular culture is used to label people who appear confident and self-assured on social media, often sharing a volume of selfies, and seem more self-involved than we would like them to be. Personally, I feel that this is less a sign of lack of empathy, than a desire for connection, for validation: we all need validation from time to time, and connection is an essential human need. When we look at people who share self-portraits, or share their lives, maybe we need to be kinder, to exercise our own empathy rather than jumping to conclusions about their motivations for sharing. We should do away with the label of 'narcissistic' because we have no real idea what is going on inside someone's head. Our culture of likes and followers can be addictive to all of us, creating feelings of inadequacy and self-loathing when we feel we don't 'measure up'.

Shame is at the root of self-loathing. Shame is one of the worst emotions we can experience, capable of killing self-esteem, confidence, and provoking unhealthy behaviours, thoughts, and relationships. Shame leaves us little room to breathe, and should be banished from any kind of discussion around bodies and food. Shame is a trigger for many of us—sending us into spirals of anxiety. Nobody should have to live with shame, to feel as if their body is somehow 'wrong'. Me and shame are old friends—I know exactly how it feels to have someone judge, insult, and make assumptions about you because of the way you look, and to be within a society that considers my type of body—curvy, fat, and squishy—as part of a 'problem' that needs a 'cure'. You can't make assumptions about someone because of the way they look. That will only lead towards disrespect and disregarding the individuality of each person.

I will touch on health briefly here. Just as there are healthy thin, or 'normal' (whatever that is!) sized people, there are healthy large, fat, and 'overweight' people. What counts is not somebody's size, but the other correlations of health measurements, such as blood sugar, cholesterol, blood pressure, and a whole gamut of other numbers that are far more important than the number on the scale. Weighing ourselves is a better measure of the way we gain and lose water in our bodies as opposed to fat. If you take that away, what you are left with is the possibility that lifestyle matters more than the number on the scale—eating well, listening to your body, moving in ways that make you happy (and in ways that you are able to), that get endorphins rushing around your body, and taking care of your mental health.

HAES (Health at Every Size) is one of the most important systems of thinking about food and nutrition to come out of the medical establishment in the last twenty years—and will most likely heal some of the disordered ways we think about food and our bodies. The books *Body Respect* (by Linda Bacon, PhD and Lucy Aphramor, PhD, RD) and *Health At Every Size* (Linda Bacon, PhD) are both good places to start to understand the real science behind the way bodies work, and don't rely on any kind of faddy, often dangerous crash diets that aren't sustainable over the long term, and often do great damage to the chemistry in the human body. Many of the so-called 'facts' we think we know about our bodies are simply deeply ingrained misinformation, rehashed by studies that are decades old and out of date. Understanding our bodies and how they work goes some way towards accepting them, caring about them, and feeling good about yourself. All the unhealthy messages and shaming that we receive from the world at large can often be remedied by looking at the body in a kinder, more fact-based way.

Conversely, bodies that are 'unhealthy', are also deserving of love, respect, and self-love. If you have an illness, or a syndrome (like me with PCOS), or any other number of issues, you are also worthy. Health is not a stick to beat yourself—or anyone else—with. Bodies are bodies, the heart and mind that live within that body, who you are, and how you love and treat others—are ultimately what matters the most. Taking care of yourself however you can, giving yourself what you need within your means—that is more important. We have this idea of 'health' as looking a certain way, when again, it's not possible for many of us to achieve the same kind of 'health' as someone who isn't dealing with or coping with particular issues.

You don't owe anybody, or the world at large, 'good' health, especially if the ways we are encouraged to attain that health are unhealthy.

When we look at image, too, I'm reminded that people within the disability community also discuss how the Western ideal doesn't include people with various disabilities, and how the lack of body diversity within our media extends to disability too. Occasionally, there is a temporary change—such as with the Paralympics, where disabled people are able to display superhuman feats of strength, agility, and speed, but society's treatment of disability relegates 'normal' disabled people to the fringes. As a society, we are still not fully comfortable with viewing people with disabilities as whole, beautiful human beings. We have to move beyond the idea of bodies as medicalised, as sites of diagnoses, and into a more holistic, accepting, and celebratory space of how amazingly, beautifully diverse human beings are. To change the cultural notions we have, we have to seek out and expose ourselves to a variety of people and their bodies, to get used to seeing bodies that don't fit this impossible ideal we are spoon-fed. To treat other people with different bodies with respect.

There are two other concepts within the body positive community that haven't been fully explored in the mainstream—body neutrality, and body liberation. Jes Baker explores body liberation in a chapter in her memoir, *Landwhale*, and I feel it is something to strive towards, especially when 'body love' feels like it is just another item on your 'to do' list. As she says, the less she forces herself to love her body, the less she hates it: 'Liberation is slowly learning how to become the best version of our whole selves—body included, yes. But it is no longer a requirement on our checklist of self-improvement to learn to love it.'

Becoming the best version of ourselves is a life-long endeavour, one in which we unlearn all the toxic messages around us about how to live in our bodies, how to treat our bodies and selves with kindness and acceptance and how to be a better person—for ourselves, for the people we love, and the community around us. That doesn't mean we have to be perfect—far from it. In essence, it is about learning to be our imperfect, messy selves, and to be okay with that.

Body neutrality, by the same token, is similar in that we don't feel the need or desire to discuss bodies in value terms—as 'good' or 'bad'. Bodies just are. They are part of our existence and what we move through the world in. No body is 'better' than any other body. Many of us move towards body neutrality, towards peace and acceptance of our bodies, rather than body love, especially when we have been participating in body dissatisfaction and diet-culture. Often, when we are striving towards loving our bodies, we are thinking too much about our bodies, when ideally, existing in our bodies without thinking too much about them is the ideal state. Too easily, the idea of body positivity can be another way for women to police their emotions, to slide from body hate to a different kind of body obsession. Body neutrality takes the pressure off, aims to gradually move towards a way of engaging in behaviours that support the body—much like body liberation—supporting us towards living in a way that feels good to us and our bodies.

I consider body positivity to be more about boosting people around me, and boosting myself in moments of uncertainty. We often think of 'love' as a happy, feel good, perfect state, when really, real love takes work, and has ups and downs. Love is not an upward tick or linear. It is kind and compassionate. I consider the body positive movement, size and body acceptance, and the fat activism community as necessary in a world that so often tells us that we're not good enough, that our bodies aren't worthy of love and respect. Yet, body liberation and body neutrality are often options that are more sustainable for everyday life and for the future. I would like to see a world in which we can all feel liberated from the toxicity surrounding us.

It takes courage to look deeply at and question what we have been taught, at the messages we get from media, advertising and the diet industry (which has an investment in keeping us yo-yo dieting so that we will need to buy more of their products). To extricate ourselves from comparing, engaging in talk that disparages our bodies, devaluing the amazing job our bodies do day by day of carrying us around, however we move. Tasting and digesting food, helping us think, and allowing us to live our lives. Our bodies are our vessel for experiencing the world. It's past time to celebrate bodies in all their diversity, and learn how to better see the beauty in that variety. To do so is to remove ourselves from self-loathing and move away from comparison culture. Let's celebrate what we can do with our bodies, rather than what we can't—and move towards body liberation. Live in the now, with the body you have.

I Sweat On The Tube

I don't just sweat on the tube, I sweat pretty much anywhere. It's not much of a confession—of course, everyone sweats sometimes. You'd be forgiven for thinking that maybe I'm exaggerating, that there is nothing remarkable about sweating on the tube, given that it's often hotter than an oven and everyone gets crammed in like sardines at rush hour. What is remarkable, though, is that I sweat on the tube even when nobody else appears to be doing so. When it's in the middle of winter and it's icy outside. The moment I step onto the tube, swaddled in a thick wool coat, scarf up to my nose, some odd chemical reaction takes place. It's almost as if all my sweat glands begin to yell in unison: 'She's on the tube! Quick, let's make every pore ooze!'

And of course, it's not just the tube. I'll be happily walking along, with aforementioned winter coat, on a freezing day. And like a magpie bedazzled by shiny trinkets, I'll see a bookshop. Naturally, I'll go inside, drawn by the scent of fresh pages, which I swear must be funnelled out onto the street through hidden air vents. I'll go in, and immediately, the heat of the radiators has my forehead leaking in no time. I become extra conscious of the leakiness, which doesn't help—sure that everyone must be wondering if the climate outside has suddenly turned tropical (they'll be sorely disappointed).

It isn't as if I smell stale or that I don't maintain my hygiene. I adore showers, deodorant, and perfume (to a fault—I used to collect perfume). My sweatiness, unfortunately, appears to be genetic. My father is also afflicted with over-excitable sweat glands and has passed it on to his daughters. Or at least, if not genetic, perhaps we are all easily stressed and over-heated. Being highly sensitive and an introvert, not to mention a little socially anxious and shy, doesn't help matters. I've done my research—not much I can do about it except keep clean, have tissues on hand, and a travel-sized bottle of deodorant with me.

Sweat glands that react quickly to changes in temperature are healthy, and it's a good sign that I'm not suffering with skin that refuses to cool itself down, otherwise known as hypohidrosis, amongst other causes (such as heatstroke). In fact, the idea of not being able to sweat—well, brings me out in a cold sweat. Humans have 2 million to 4 million sweat glands, and we are born with them—the number doesn't change. In theory, sweat should eventually evaporate. The sweat that produces a scent is found under the armpit (along with some other parts of the human body), and usually results from the naturally occurring bacteria on our bodies reacting with sweat produced from the apocrine sweat glands (which also produces yellow stains). Most of our sweat is otherwise salty but odourless and colour-less. When we consider that our bodies are on average, around 50-70% water, we are carrying around an inbuilt water-cooler. Most mammals also have the ability to cool themselves down—cats sweat from their paws, for example.

For women, though, there is an extra stigma connected to sweating. Deodorant ads typically seem to push the idea of women sweating being a disaster, or at least an unfeminine state. There's a fine line being walked between pushing a product aimed at stopping sweat, or at least covering up sweat, and presenting the impossible image of a woman who hardly breaks a sweat even when running for the bus (or the tube). So, when we do see women who sweat a lot, or even just a little, we are either conditioned to be covertly horrified, or think she isn't looking after herself. When the reverse is true—sweating is a sign that our bodies are working to cool themselves, and some people simply sweat more than others. It is seen as undesirable and oddly, unnatural. There is a point to be made here about how female bodies are subject to public social and cultural disapproval—how the natural functioning of our bodies is seen as shameful.

Whilst I don't feel particularly comfortable or attractive when my body decides to have a freak-out moment, at least I know that it is just trying to make me feel cooler. Training ourselves to be less concerned with what other people think, goes some way towards addressing the stigma surrounding the (often hidden) functioning of our bodies. Sometimes, it's hard to remind ourselves that everyone has embarrassing moments with their bodies, but it's humbling to remember that not everything our bodies do is under our control. Control is a cultural (and political) concept, wrapped up in what is considered 'polite' and 'nice'. If women are pressured to be quiet, to take up less space, to 'control' themselves and their bodies, sweating is one of those ways in which our bodies express the ultimate 'lack of control'. Liberating ourselves from the stigma of a culture that believes female bodies should be hairless, smooth, sweat-free, and a myriad of other unattainable characteristics, is the goal—and accepting that we are often sweaty creatures is a part of that.

In fact, apart from hot summer days and sunshine, I blame the over-heating of everything. In the winter, every shop cranks up the heating, it feels, to the highest setting. And of course, the tube. Airless, miles underground, and packed with hundreds of people, no wonder my body decides that it would rather be covered in water than become overheated. Even in the spring, shops and cafés can be a veritable sauna—after coming in from a damp, humid day, you are greeted with the uncomfortable sense that you've walked into a greenhouse. On those in-between days when you've left the house with a coat on, you will feel that you'd rather be in sandals. And it isn't just my forehead that sweats—my head sweats too. So as well as looking like it's 30 degrees outside, I also give the impression that it's been raining.

I miss bathrooms that have hand-dryer vents that turn upwards. Remember those? Instead now, we have these super-technological laser-stream hot air contraptions, which are no use at all for drying hair that has been subjected to sweat glands. In these situations, it is best to scruff your hair up and blot away with tissues, doing your best to not look like someone who's just been swimming. The only thing that seems to help is shucking all the layers I've decided to wear in my infinite (!) wisdom, put my hair up, take my scarf off, and hope for the best.

I'm not one of those people who worships the summer months— I'm a spring and autumn person. Summer, for me, means damage control. It means assembling a super-kit of face powder, blotting pads (my hero product), deodorant, tissues, hairbands, water-spray, an extra thin cover-up just in case what I'm wearing needs to be changed or covered, and a large bottle of water—all the water coming out needs to go back in again, of course. Luckily, in the summer, the amount of people sweating increases dramatically, so at least I know I'm not suffering alone in my own puddle. And sandals are incredible—I can't imagine what summer would be like without a soft breeze cooling my toes. My ideal climate would be somewhere between spring and autumn, when there is still sunlight and warmth but a cooling sea-breeze. My fantasy is eventually semi-retiring with my husband to a seaside town, just as many people living in big cities often fantasise about.

It's come to the point in my life now where I'm considering whether I should care about what other people think, or whether I should carry on my anxious ways of worrying about what other people think about my sweatiness. The conclusion I've come to is even though there are times when being a sweaty-Betty is more of a concern, the people who care the most in my life just aren't bothered if they get to see my shiny forehead. I care less and less about whether or not I'm sweating on the tube. I see other people sweating too—and since I know that the tube is a terrible, unnatural environment for the human body, I just feel solidarity that we are surviving the journey.

Getting rid of that anxiety often does solve the sweatiness itself, though it doesn't solve those moments of sardine-heat or over-zealous radiator usage. The cultural messages around sweat have confused us—it isn't dirty, unnatural, or something that we have any control over: in fact it is important to understand why we sweat and how it aids the functioning of our bodies, because if anything, it's fascinating that we have the capacity to cool ourselves down. And if you—too—sweat on the tube (or anywhere else)—you're not alone.

On Health and Radical Body Positivity

In '*Body Positivity*', I wrote about the practice of body positivity and how we are all enough, and that all bodies are valid: no body is better than any other body. We are all worthy of our own appreciation and the love and respect of others. Yet, you might find yourself continuing the refrain of 'but what if that person's health is at risk?' or 'what if I'm not 'healthy'?'

First, I'm obviously not a qualified doctor, nor am I an expert by any means. I only know what I've learnt over the years, and what I'm currently learning about health, from reading, and from observing the relationship I have and other people have, with the concept of 'health'. In countries such as the UK, US, and Europe, health is equated with a particular 'look'—thin, white, and with glowing (often tanned) skin. Obviously the problematic thing here is that it excludes a range of cultures, backgrounds, and abilities, not to mention other body shapes and sizes. It is simply not a realistic image: usually these images are highly photoshopped, involve lighting and make-up, and in some extreme cases, look nothing like the flesh and blood people they are supposed to depict.

Denigrating our own bodies is often seen as a way to bond within groups of women—for example, 'I feel so fat today' or 'does my bum look big in this', or even 'I'd love to look like her/be as thin as her.' Food talk tends towards the guilty kind of talk—feeling as if we're being 'bad' by eating something, or that we'll have to 'make up for it' tomorrow by not eating 'so much'.

Personally, I find this kind of talk triggering. I know that other people do too. I used to have a difficult relationship with food when I was younger. Having struggles at secondary school around communication, friendships, shyness, and anxiety made my relationship with food sketchy. I saw it as an emotional crutch in times of stress and worry—in particular, chocolate was my favourite mood booster.

During this period, the talk around me with women who were my role models and peers tended towards ideas of weight loss, of crash diets, or depriving themselves in some way. I constantly felt inadequate and unattractive, and food was a source of both pleasure and guilt. Luckily, I didn't slide into purging or starving myself, but often it was touch and go.

Most diet-talk tends towards using guilt and shame. Guilt and shame erode people's self-worth and self-esteem. Our relationship with our bodies is personal and intimate, and when we bring shame and guilt to that relationship, it's a recipe for disaster. This is why, to change the way we connect with our bodies, we need radical body positivity, to replace these feelings of guilt and shame. Removing them from the conversation means that we are able to then breathe and move towards a healthier—mentally, emotionally, and physically—relationship with our bodies. I don't mean 'healthy' in the narrow way prescribed by society, but in a way that feels good to you.

Being a woman with PCOS (polycystic ovarian syndrome), I've found that it's taken me many years to get to a point where I've become more positive and empowered about my condition. Being diagnosed with PCOS, something that is largely misunderstood and which requires a great deal of self-advocacy, researching, and experimentation, means that you have to learn to make peace with your body, and accept it, whilst at the same time making positive changes that will help manage the condition.

The current research points to PCOS being an autoimmune inflammatory and metabolic syndrome. Some of the difficult symptoms can be weight gain (and difficulty managing that due to the complicated hormone imbalances), excess hair growth (hirsutism), irregular or absent periods, insulin resistance, anxiety, depression, sugar and carbohydrate cravings, and aches and pains. Not all women, however, have the same symptoms, and to make the situation even more confusing, there are about four different types with a different constellation of symptoms.

In bringing this up, I'm trying to express how complicated it is to have a human body. We don't know for sure how a body will react to an environment, lifestyle, or life circumstances. No two bodies will react to the same lifestyle in the same way—what makes one person feel good won't make another feel good. Our bodies aren't machines—they're a complicated collection of cells, organs, neurons, pathways, muscles, and bones. It mirrors how complicated the human psyche is. I have certain 'triggers' for my feelings of guilt, depression, and anxiety, just as anyone does.

Radical body positivity calls for me to use a holistic way of looking after my body. That means using food as medicine (as well as fuel, nutrition, and pleasure), looking at the foods that cause or exacerbate inflammation, the activities that will help my cells use insulin properly, and the self-care routines and rituals that will help me reduce stress in my life. It avoids looking at food as something that I should feel guilty about, that there aren't 'bad' and 'good' foods, just that some foods, if not eaten in moderation, may cause blood sugar spikes and make me ill. The goal here is to give my body the best possible chance of healing and balancing, to support my organs and the processes going on around them.

I don't believe that food is inherently good or bad. It just is. Of course, food that is overly processed is going to have some nutritional deficiencies (and some food is so processed that it doesn't look like the original product it started as), but ultimately, food is fuel, and it can also be a great pleasure. I enjoy food—I don't always have the energy to enjoy cooking it—some days it's more of a chore—but a delicious meal is one of the best joys in life. Food can bring people together, it can transport you to another place, it can comfort, heal, and bring you to life. It holds memories and culture.

Part of body positivity is celebrating difference, and non-judgement of people's lifestyles. We are all responsible for our bodies and what we choose to do, or not do, with them. In UK and US culture, we attach too much value and judgement to situations that are often outside of our control—resulting in disablist and sizeist attitudes. We are allowed to talk about our bodies how we want to talk about them, but maybe we need to be more mindful of how we talk about bodies around other people. Being conscious of our biases and prejudices. No body is better than another body. That is the essence of body positivity – that no body is better than any other, and we all have a right to celebrate and exist in a variety of bodies, without fear of judgement or prejudice.

Health can also be something wielded in a way that excludes and compounds inequalities. For example, not everyone has the financial means to access relevant healthcare, or pursue the kind of healthcare they have a right to receive. Not everyone has the space to store fresh food, or the time to make it. If you give up a certain type of food or drink, or make certain changes in your diet, it doesn't mean that your morality is better than someone else's. It may be a controversial attitude to take, and I respect the choices people make regarding religion, or changes made in consideration of the environment, animal welfare, or lifestyle, but none of us are better than anyone else because of those choices. Food is also political—if fresh food was cheaper than ready-made, pre-packaged foods, we would find that more people might be drawn to eating a wider range of different foods. Instead, raising the costs of pre-packaged foods (such as ready meals or sweet foods) and not also reducing the costs of fresh food, will ultimately mean that people on lower incomes will become poorer.

In *Body Respect*, a book by Linda Bacon and Lucy Aphramor, they write about how class, social inequality, and the stress and oppression that comes with being in a low income household can also contribute to illness, stress-related problems, and lack of good-quality nutrition. Oppression, through economic, racial, disability, and other myriad factors, can affect health. The way different identity markers interact can change the way you access healthcare, what kind of food you are able to afford: your economic background can greatly influence your body size, metabolism, mental health, and fitness. The point that Bacon and Aphramor make is that the mental stress of discrimination, poverty, and systematic oppression mean that our bodies also come under an immense amount of stress: 'The issue is not simply one of income, though it is important to consider the realities of material deprivation. Nor is it differences in lifestyle—whether you smoke or eat a daily doughnut. It is the experience of inequality—how much control you have over your life and the opportunities you have—that plays a profound role in health and longevity.'

Moving away from food, movement and exercise have also been used to compound inequalities. Not everyone enjoys or can access conventional means of movement (such as gym memberships, sports, access to green spaces, or movement geared towards people without disabilities). Anxiety and depression can get in the way of someone enjoying or taking part in the kinds of movement they want to do. Yet, enjoying your own body and the kinds of movement it can do, adapting your environment and the tools you use, is part of radical body positivity. Rather than aiming for arbitrary and stressful goals, we can just aim to have fun, to have a better relationship with our bodies, and to use exercise to reduce stress in our lives.

Maybe the aim should be to try as many different sports and types of movement as you can, to find activities that you enjoy doing. I don't believe that exercise should be a chore, or something that, again, holds some kind of moral meaning. Whether you do or don't exercise shouldn't matter in terms of personal worth. It can boost mood, make you feel more relaxed, and connect you more to the present, but it isn't a moral competition. Exercise doesn't need to be a means to an end. Often, people believe that exercise can lead to long-term weight loss, and when it doesn't, they feel demotivated.

Far better then, to see movement as something that is part of a joyful life, that gives us myriad benefits beyond reaching some kind of ideal weight. We know that movement offers benefits to our mental health, body chemistry, energy, and overall sense of wellbeing. As Bacon and Aphramor put it: 'The projected weight impact doesn't motivate most people to stay active. People who exercise regularly tend to do so because it gives them an enormous sense of well-being. They feel more energetic throughout the day, sleep better at night, have sharper memories and clearer minds, and feel more relaxed and positive about themselves and their lives. And it doesn't take hours of pumping weights in a gym or running mile after mile to achieve those results.'

Remembering the joy you felt as a child, swimming, going for bike rides around the park, swinging on the swings, and jumping as high as possible on trampolines is a great place to start. Movement is about making the time for joy and relaxation, even when sometimes, getting to the point where you feel good can be hard work. The mindset we bring to exercise, that of accepting and celebrating our bodies and what they can do, as opposed to what they can't, goes a long way towards fostering joy in our range of movement. Instead of berating yourself for how little exercise you feel you've done, or whether you feel you worked hard enough, instead aim for enjoying activity as a way to make yourself feel good. Do what you can when you can—fit activity into your life because you want to. Once again, as Bacon and Aphramor have said: 'The research shows that switching focus to pleasurable movement (play!), health gain, and body attunement is far more effective in supporting a sustained increase in activity level than a focus on exercise for weight loss. You'll notice this definition of what we can think of as "realistic fitness" applies equally well to someone with limited mobility as it does to an elite athlete.'

Self-care and radical body positivity are practices that continue throughout your whole life—they will always be philosophies that need working on. You're not going to always have a love-love relationship with your body, and aiming for neutral acceptance is often better. In the end, what matters is that you consider letting go of the narrow, restrictive, and often negative view of health as a moral imperative. Each of us has a unique body that is worth looking after—for you, nobody else. How you do that is between you and yourself, with the resources you have. You don't need to look like anyone but yourself, and don't have to do the same as anyone else either.

Fatshion and Taking Up Space

There is no avoiding the fact that we all have to clothe ourselves. Some of us like to wear garments that express something about us, whether that is identity, a sense of fun, a sub-culture, an appreciation of colour and style in general, or that we simply like wearing cardigans. For others, it's just a matter of practicality, of clothes that fit well and serve a purpose.

The women in my family have always seemed to enjoy a sense of style with clothes. My Granny was always neat and smart, and I never saw her wear jogging bottoms or a well-loved oversized jumper. She, and her cousin Marjorie (who we called Auntie Marjorie), always wore lipstick for special occasions, or just to leave the house, and I always thought that was glamorous. My Mum has a lovely sense of style, and growing up I've seen it change with her different decades, and have seen how it's possible to adapt your own style.

Sarah, my sister, and I have very different approaches to style. Hers is much more modern bohemian, whilst I have sort of veered towards pretty dresses, fun vintage and modern prints, cat-eye glasses, brogues and boots, and of course my impressive addiction to a good cardigan. I hold on to clothes long past their wearability because they remind me of good times, or because I still stubbornly think that this fraying beloved cardigan can hold up to one more wear. I believe in the power of a piece of clothing to change how you feel on a bad day, to give you confidence when you need it, and to feel a sense of comfort.

Having said that, for the longest time, clothes were my worst enemy. Or at least shopping would end in a sense of self-loathing, deep dissatisfaction, and at the worst, betrayal. I don't believe that anyone should be made to feel bad about going to the shops if they want or need a piece of clothing. I feel that it reflects badly on a shop if they refuse to stock a wide range of sizing, small and large, and everything in-between, and that modern sizing is completely arbitrary and varies from shop to shop anyway. Especially for those of us who have bodies considered plus size, a UK size 16-32 and upwards. Never mind that the average size in womenswear in the UK is actually a 14 or 16.

When I was a teenager, I felt intense shame about my body. The messages I received damaged my perception of how my body looked, to the extent that I believed my body was somehow wrong. The shops that my friends shopped in, Miss Selfridge and Topshop, Dorothy Perkins, and H&M, didn't often have clothes I could wear that I actually liked. When I did find something that fit and that I liked, I was incandescently happy. I think most girls feel this way, especially with their first forays into style and self-identity. I didn't have a svelte body, it was curvy and had a few lumps and bumps, and in hindsight I should have felt confident enough to try bigger sizes, to look in shops that I wouldn't otherwise think of trying, but when you're young, sometimes you want to fit in a little.

My way of fitting in was to accessorise. Bags, shoes, jewellery, nail polish, and lip-gloss. If I couldn't wear the same sort of clothes that my friends wore, I would rock the platform trainers and the dark blue nail polish. I pierced my ears in three places. I enjoyed the clothes I did have, and learnt that the same outfit could look different with clever accessorising. This is what many plus size teens did in the 90s and 00s. We had a love affair with shoes and jewellery.

They gave us a way of expressing the colour of our identities, and identifying with our friends.

At some point, some shops did begin to branch out their sizing, and recognise that there was a market for plus size ranges. Online shopping meant that there was a little more choice. It was around 2009 that I truly began to have fun with style and fashion, and set up a blog so I could participate in the fledgling 'fatshion' community. These were the days of DIY mirror outfit of the day shots, before anyone started using DSLRs and asking their boyfriends or friends to take their photos. It was an exciting time to be a plus size woman or man, to understand that we had a right to claim our own identities and bodies, and define ourselves in a positive, empowering way. Brands took notice of blogs and began to make clothes that suited a range of bodies and styles.

Identity politics were emerging, though I had been aware of fat acceptance and body acceptance for a while beforehand through the Women's Studies department at university. A postgraduate student doing her doctorate specialised in Fat Studies, studying representations and identities of fat bodies, reclaiming the word 'fat' as a descriptor rather than loaded with negative connotations. It was liberating, and it started me on the road towards understanding that it is possible to accept your body and debunk myths surrounding bodies that are different. Celebrating what your body can do, rather than what it can't do, to at least remove judgement from the way we experience bodies.

I know that it might be a controversial idea for people to understand. We live in a society that has a scare sign above it in neon letters: 'Obesity Crisis'. Size, however, is not an indicator of someone's health; you can be fat and fit, with good numbers, and small with a host of health issues. I'm not arguing that health doesn't matter—looking after yourself, mentally and physically, is a personal undertaking (and I advocate Health at Every Size, HAES). Instead, I'm talking about perception, and acceptance of a range of body sizes—and how an individual's worth is not connected to the size of their body. There are all kinds of damaging stigmas different societies attach to bodies like mine—that we are slow and stupid, that we are lazy, that we don't care about health, figures of fun, and that somehow we are worth less than smaller people. We attach value to size, as if it is the measure of someone's humanity.

The 'fatshion' blogging community was, and still is, all about the celebration of bodies of every size and shape. It was about reclaiming the word 'fat' as a descriptor, even if you chose not to use that descriptor for yourself. It was about holding each other up, subversively wearing all the clothes that so-called style gurus said we shouldn't—horizontal stripes, pencil dresses, bright colours, even bikinis! It was the origin of the question and answer: 'how do you get a bikini body?' 'Put a bikini on it.' It became a space where we wrote about what it was like to live in our bodies, the various types of discrimination and oppression we experienced, and it allowed us to take up space in the world, to be unapologetic. It takes courage to not apologise for taking up space when your body is big. Especially for women and female-identified people, who are meant to somehow shrink ourselves to take up less space than men do. We are discouraged from taking up space and having loud voices, from being obtrusive and having opinions, from being angry about things that we should all be angry about. Anger can be channelled into action, and sometimes, actions change life for the better.

These days, I am most comfortable wearing dresses, which is a complete about-turn from how I used to be when I was young. If you told me when I was a teenager that I'd be able to feel comfortable, be able to choose to wear what I want to wear, and that I would be able to express myself by wearing dresses of all kinds, I would be incredulous—but of course I would have raided adult-me's wardrobe. Trousers and jeans are also available in my size, and in larger sizes, which is a good marker of progress in plus size fashion. However, most mainstream high street shops still vary in their offerings to plus size customers. Imagine the money they would make if they opened up their sizing and had a rush of stylish people buying their clothes? It makes little business sense to limit the sizing of your clothing. For example, Fat Face only goes up to a size 18, the same as Zara and Topshop.

Often, even the range of sizes in these shops run small, so women of all sizes will end up sizing up. The fashion industry as a whole does have a problem with accommodating different body types and sizes, so unfortunately, plus size teens may still have trouble shopping for clothes that fit well. ASOS has Curve, and River Island also has a stylish plus size range, so there is still reason to hope that other high street retailers will take note. It is the independent brands that are being inclusive and creative, offering a wider range of sizes. I've bought clothes from places like Scarlet and Jo and Lady V Vintage, and if you do some investigating online, there are always some surprising options in plus sizing. The great thing about being open minded is that you can often find garments in straight-size shops that fit because they are stretchy or because they have extra material. Some knitwear can fit larger sizes, and t-shirts can be generous. Ultimately, you end up learning to try clothes on, no matter what the size on the label says.

Once you begin to see bodies as just that—bodies—which come in every shape and size—you can focus on enjoying your life and your body, being good to yourself, and appreciating what you can do. Detach any kind of value judgement from different bodies, and you can see people for who they are. Bodies come in all sizes and abilities, and everyone has their own beauty and worth.

Living As Woman

Having written about hair, sweat, and body positivity, you would think there is little else to write about living as a woman—a particular woman; white, cisgender, deaf, in her thirties, with access to the NHS. It's a long story though, the tale of women's bodies, and there is always some other detail and fact to impart.

At this moment in time, Hollywood has imploded, with the 'Time to Change' and 'Me Too' campaigns—the not-so-secret world of sexual violence, intimidation, and coercion exposed for all to see. A few years ago, Everyday Feminism, run by Laura Bates, documented the microaggressions and everyday acts of sexism and misogyny women experience. The slow, steady work of change is ongoing.

All women live with fear of violence. I know that we live in uncertain times, with worries about terrorist attacks and fragile diplomatic relationships on the international stage. The fact remains, though, that in the US, for example, a woman is beaten every nine seconds, and there is a reported rape every 6.2 minutes—and one in five women is raped in her lifetime, according to statistics gleaned from Rebecca Solnit's book *Men Explain Things To Me*. Groups of men, no matter how benign, are viewed with suspicion, particularly if they have been drinking. I will cross over the road at night if I'm walking alone, and a man approaches, or is walking behind me. As a deaf woman, I am doubly on alert—watching shadows, walking quickly, ready to run if I need to. This is in a society and culture that is relatively safe. Except it isn't, not quite. Every woman I know has experienced some kind of issue with men, with consent, with assault or coercion. I've had experiences in broad daylight when my body has been violated, out of the blue, for no other reason than I'm female shaped.

The importance of respect and consent cannot be over-stated. No means no, women are people, and there are no grey areas. Sometimes women aren't sure themselves what constitutes consent, especially if they find themselves in situations where the imbalance of power makes it difficult. These conditions don't mean consent—being naked, kissing, wearing revealing clothes, being drunk, inviting someone in, being invited in. Consent is when you are all in, when you agree to an encounter, when you want to be touched a certain way. At any point during an encounter—for both men and women and any other gender—you are allowed to say no. If anything makes you uncomfortable in any way, no is no. Even if that person is your long-time partner, husband, wife—you're allowed to say no, because it's your body and your mind. Nobody has ownership over your body.

This is the real issue within many societies, the idea of bodies as objects which we 'do' things to, shells that are visited upon. When bodies aren't objects. What we experience with our bodies is part of our life experience. Any trauma, operations, activity, pleasure, or pain that we experience becomes part of our mental and emotional landscape. Being a deaf woman, I understand this deeply, because my deafness—the physical fact of it, and the associated identity surrounding it—is a part of who I am. There are scars on my body from operations, marks on my skin from blisters, a couple of burns, bad falls—bodies are maps of experience. They are not separate objects that can be visited upon without any effect.

This is why the epidemic of violence against women and our

bodies is so insidious. It isn't violence against objects, against bodies that have no feeling, that are separate from the people this violence is done to. It has lasting trauma, mushrooms out to friends, family, communities. Women are automatically questioned about their experiences, instead of being listened to, and the dismal imprisonment rate and short sentences for sexual violence and rape is a cosmic, but very real, joke. Women-identified people make up 52 per cent of the world's population—2 per cent more than half—and yet our bodies are still seen as less than human. No other explanation quite makes sense—why else would the violence, not just literal violence, but images, films, media, language—have reached epidemic proportions, even in societies that are purportedly 'equal'?

There's a bigger conversation to be had about sexuality and toxic masculinity that hasn't quite emerged yet from the mainstream media in the wake of the 'Time's Up' and 'Me Too' campaigns. About how sexual harassment, rape, coercion, and street harassment are part of a wider culture of entitlement and objectification. The kind of culture where small everyday incidents of sexism are so commonplace that despite knowing they are wrong, sometimes we can't be bothered to comment on them, reserving our energy protesting larger, supposedly more impactful incidents.

Yet these small microaggressions build up. If we live in a world where we can't protest these smaller instances (such as mansplaining, not being listened to, being passed over for promotion, the pay gap, catcalling, and so on), maybe we're all accepting mediocrity and reinforcing the idea that women are second class citizens. Whilst not violence visited on our bodies, they still stem from the idea that women are somehow less. That our contributions to society and the world of work, our presence in public spaces, and our minds and voices, are not as essential as men's. If we—both women and men—accept that and don't believe it is worth changing, then we will continue to live in a world where it's acceptable to have a predator as a president, and for the lives of countless women—and men—men are also victims of male on male sexual and emotional violence, and violence also takes place in gay and lesbian relationships—to be lost in this 'hidden' war of sexual violence and abuse.

Feminism is a complicated movement, because it has often excluded women of colour, disabled women, transgender people, and working-class women. With the rise of intersectional feminism, some of these balances have been addressed, but there is still some way to go yet before feminism as a movement will learn from the past. Intersectional feminism is feminism that recognises that markers of social discrimination, such as class, race, sexual orientation, age, disability, body size, and gender, are not separate but woven together, having an impact on a person and groups of people according to their social markers. For example, I have had a middle-class upbringing, I'm white, and cisgender—my gender identity matches my birth sex—but I am also deaf, and experience life as a plus sized woman. This means I experience different oppressions, social and structural inequalities and barriers that other people may not experience.

Regardless, feminism is an important movement, because it's all about fighting for liberation, for all. Liberation from patriarchy—the pervasive structural and cultural system that holds that women are second class citizens. Patriarchy hurts men in a number of ways too, from toxic masculinity that tells men that they must behave in a certain way to be accepted by society (lack of emotion, aggressive, objectifying, showing no 'weakness') to short periods of paternity leave (if there is any offered at all).

Men may benefit in various ways from patriarchy, but if you consider how toxic masculinity works—by treating human emotions as weakness, often by using aggression and addictive substances (alcohol, drugs) to cope with emotion—overwhelmingly, men are more likely to abuse substances. Men, therefore, are less likely to seek help for mental health struggles, and there is some

47

evidence to suggest that the high male suicide rate in the UK and US can be linked to men feeling unable to talk about what they are going through. Rigid gender norms are just as dangerous for men as they are for women.

Learning to be intelligent about emotions, being empathetic, and talking about mental health is not weak. Our society views femininity as weakness, when realistically, personality traits and healthy behaviours should be free of being pigeonholed as 'masculine' or 'feminine'. Men stepping up and being more involved in childcare and household management is another way that patriarchy limits the roles men can play within the family. Men being house-husbands, for example, or sharing the housework and day to day running of the house with their (often female) partners, is still seen as emasculating, when it is a necessary thing in an equal world. These kind of discussions around what it means to be a man in an equal partnership, in a world where we all treat each other with respect, need to happen for a better future for everyone.

At the level of the body, women's bodies are still political battlegrounds. Issues such as family planning and contraception, the period tax (tax on sanitary products), abortion (particularly in Ireland and Northern Ireland and the US, amongst many other countries), and women's health are constantly being controlled by and debated by rooms full of men. Unlike men's health issues, which are treated as inalienable rights, women are constantly having to fight for their right to have ownership over their own bodies. I've written countless letters to my local MP about some of these issues, when legislation has gone through parliament eroding some of women's rights. You would expect that legislation is set in stone, but different parties have differing agendas and will seek to amend bills, even rights that seem like they could never be changed.

Sexuality is also something that can be complicated when you live as a woman. Whatever your sexual preferences, as I mentioned before, consent can be difficult to navigate and sexual autonomy and freedom can be difficult to practice. Women are entitled to sexual safety and pleasure, and from what I can remember of sex education at secondary school, only one of those was addressed (types of contraception – in the science lab!), and only in the context of heterosexuality. Consent wasn't discussed, and neither was women's health discussed in any further detail than scientifically outlining symptoms of sexually transmitted infections and diseases. Women's sexuality wasn't, and conventionally isn't, discussed as separate to male sexuality. It is taken as a given that because we're seen as two opposites in terms of biology, that women's desires and anatomy are therefore complementary to men's. There was no discussion of female masturbation (still a taboo subject, even in the twenty-first century after Sex and the City almost ten years ago!), orgasm, asexuality, or homosexuality.

Quite honestly, sex education at most schools is an anatomy lesson, which has less to do with human affection and desires, and the safe, intimate, and consenting encounters that good sex should aim to be, and more to do with the way we, as a society, view sex to be something that is 'done' to women, and often shameful. It's surrounded by the language of shame and there is a lack of open discourse about what safe sex and intimacy really looks like. Shame and guilt mean that we find it difficult to have open, mature conversations about sexuality and pleasure. Teenagers and young adults still have bad sexual encounters, sometimes unsafe, and there is a lack of open, good information. Secondary schools, and the last year of primary schools, should be the first place where we learn about safe sex and sexuality.

Teens are less likely to make costly and heart-breaking mistakes if they have access to good information. Abstinence might be a good idea in theory, but as human beings, we are always going to have desires and urges that we need to understand and make sense of. Unfortunately, with this lack of information, girls may find themselves in situations where they don't know that they are allowed to say no at any time, and boys will believe that their sexuality has to be forceful.

The idea that 'sex sells' is another thing that warps our ideas of intimacy and sexuality. Women are seen as performers, who have to look and behave a certain way in the bedroom that aligns with what is seen in the movies (or from male-aimed pornography, which is usually violent and objectifying). Sex becomes a commodity, just another thing to manipulate people with, in order to sell us a certain highly edited and dehumanised version of sexuality. The lack of intimacy, warmth, and messiness that is a part of human interaction is missing. The problematic thing is that young men often only learn about sex and sexuality from consuming this kind of media, and conversely, are directly seeing sex as something that objectifies and dehumanises both women and men.

Women's sexuality is separate from men's. It might make people feel uncomfortable thinking of female sexuality as something powerful and unique in its own right, but it's definitely possible, and often necessary in terms of safety, for women to have a happy and pleasurable sexual life without men. Not just in the context of being in relationships with other women, but as a whole, women have the capacity to have a good sexual life as individuals. Humans have a vast imagination and plenty of tools at their disposal. And if women have sexuality separate from men, so do men themselves, whatever their sexual preference. It's not an original idea, but not one that we are taught about or learn in the mainstream. Can seeing human sexuality this way lead to a greater respect of women as independent human beings, in charge of their own bodies?

In the meantime, being a woman means that we live with the fear—no matter how peripheral to our lives—of violence. Men can do a lot to reduce that fear and challenge other men on their behaviour and attitudes towards women. For example, challenging the language they use, violent or distasteful 'jokes', and touching a woman without consent, pursuing after a no, or harassing women.

Men might not want to 'rock the boat' with their friends or even family members, but as a society, we need to understand that sometimes, preventing violence against women (and men) begins with small actions like these. Use your privilege as a man in the best possible way. Being role models for children, behaving respectfully towards women, and listening to the women in your lives. Understanding that verbal and physical abuse are two sides of the same coin.

Yes, women can also take precautionary measures to avoid the possibility of sexual violence, such as basic self-defence, but the onus should be on men to challenge and take notice of what the men around them do and say. The way we dress, how much we've had to drink, or anything else that has been cited as a so-called 'provocation' for sexual violence has nothing to do with the behaviour of perpetrators. The responsibility of sexual violence lies squarely on the shoulders of the people who commit that violence and harassment. The survivors and victims of these crimes need our support and for us to stop questioning their version of events. With 'Time's Up' and 'Me Too', we can hope that such a high-profile movement filters through wider society and creates some lasting change and awareness for all of us.

Brain Music

My brain likes to sing to itself. It began when I started to lose more of my hearing, this incessant ringing, buzzing, echoing noise in my head. The audiologists gave it a name—tinnitus—but it didn't change how I would stay awake in the dark, the ringing reaching a crescendo whilst the adrenaline kicked in. How can you banish the phantoms in your head, when they show no signs of leaving? Coupled with an active childhood imagination, these noises became the monsters under the bed and in the wardrobe.

The more hearing I lost, the more the sounds varied in pitch. My brain was trying to compensate for the high and low sounds it could no longer hear. It became a monstrous orchestra. I couldn't reconcile these noises with myself, as something harmless that my body was producing. It was only as I began my lifelong musical education that my brain latched upon sounds that it could recognise.

It began with Michael Jackson's *Thriller* album. Mid childhood-tantrum, my Dad brought me a tape, leaving me to sulk with the sounds of *Beat It*, *Man in the Mirror*, and *Thriller* playing on repeat. The clean rhythms, lyrical novelty, and music that I simply fell in love with, gave my brain something else to focus on besides its own phantom echoes. At the same time, something strange began to happen with the sounds themselves. My brain trained itself to tune the noises to music, whether from my favourite movie scores (like *Star Wars*), or music snippets from shows I had performed in at Chickenshed. My mind developed its own library, constantly latching on to anything musical that sounded good.

I retained my auditory memory when I had a further few drops in hearing, so all these musical memories stayed stored in my brain. Though it became harder to pick up music in the same way without more effort on my part, music became an intrinsic part of my everyday life. As a teenager, the sounds in my brain inspired me to write my own lyrics, constantly writing bad angsty poetry and finding rhythms and melodies that came out of nowhere. As a young adult, I used music as stress relief, for celebration, as background to working, and I stayed actively looking for new styles and bands.

It has always been an active process, learning new music. It begins with listening to the song a number of times, getting used to the melody and rhythms, and looking up the lyrics or using a lyrics program to sync the music with the lyrics. Spotify was a great application when it had MusiXmatch, but I use it less than I did since they parted ways. I've discovered old favourites, as well as new ones. Yet it can be difficult to sustain that active engagement unless I make the time for it. It doesn't stop me from listening to compilations and genre focused playlists, and sometimes a song will sound good enough for me to take that next step and get to know it better.

At one point, I was convinced I had 'auditory hallucinations', but recently I've realised that this is probably not the case. My brain is actively pulling out music from memory, and setting that music to the pitches and noises in my head, even though this often happens without any conscious effort on my part. There are moments when I'm not paying attention when the tinnitus flattens out into normal ringing and pitchy tones. Auditory hallucinations are sounds that come from nowhere, that might sound like anything from sirens to music. Since I actively tune the noises to music, I doubt these can be described as auditory hallucinations under the current definition, even though the sound is within my brain and involves the tinnitus.

My family has always loved music. My parents came of age in the 1960s, and my Dad is a passionate Rolling Stones and rock music fan, whilst my Mum is a fan of The Beatles (amongst many other bands and singers). The kind of experiences they had when they were younger—going to impromptu concerts in Cambridge where they lived at the time to see everyone from the Stones to Pink Floyd—is unheard of in these days of overinflated ticket prices. In their late teens and early twenties, they were 'weekend hippies', going to concerts at the weekend whilst working during the week.

On the other hand, my Mum's Dad, affectionately named Pop, played the organ, and had a small organ in his study at my grandparent's bungalow. He would listen to Sinatra, Billie Holiday, and other greats, but also loved his film scores, particularly science fiction film scores. He would do the lighting and sound effects for the village pantomimes every year. Then there was also my uncle Peter (we called him Pete Darling) who co-owned a record shop in Kings Cross, Mole Jazz. There was no escaping the musical influences surrounding myself and my sister—and perhaps even because we are deaf, music made more of an impression on us than it would on other young children.

When I lost more of my hearing as a young teen, I tried to compensate for that by getting used to my favourite music again, playing it over many times. The lyric and poetry writing may have been another way to keep my connection to music, and redefine it on my own terms. It is difficult to know how much I can or can't hear because to me, in the end that is not the point. Of course, technically (and medically) speaking, I probably only now hear a certain percentage of the music I'm listening to—not much at all of high and low frequencies, and I challenge myself by listening to music that I supposedly shouldn't be able to enjoy, such as classical music, jazz vocals, and acoustic.

I've always described the way I listen to music as hearing the melody, bass line, some of the instruments and a voice or voices singing, but without 'making out' the words. There is something about certain pieces of music I can connect to emotionally, just as hearing people do. Though there are some genres and songs I can't connect to as well as I can with others, that is always the case with music anyway, and hearing people have their likes, dislikes, and preferences. Even so, I enjoy a wide range of different sounds, though I don't like heavy electronica or anything that sounds too 'messy'.

Some people just don't enjoy music whether deaf or hearing, and like anything, it's a preference and not essential for a happy life. It's a pleasure that enhances my existence. Just as much as I love it, I do go long stretches of time without listening to anything, even though I barely notice how much time has passed—since my brain is constantly lit up with music. Imagine carrying your own personal jukebox around with you—it is both wonderful and can also be unbearably annoying when you just wish for silence. The irritating aspect of it happens when my brain becomes stuck in a loop with one particular tune, an earworm that just won't leave. Just as much as I enjoy my connection with music, it can be something that plays up when I don't appreciate it.

Music itself is an experience that is surrounded by mythos, something that can be linked as far back as human beings have been on earth. The most primal form of music is the rhythm of the heart, the heart beating in time with the pumping of blood. It makes sense that, whether hearing or deaf, that rhythm can be felt, heard, and understood the world over. Sound doesn't need to be heard to be a part of us, with the rush of blood around our bodies. Whether or not you enjoy music, it is intrinsically a part of human experience and history. It can soothe us or wake us up, can release us from pent up energy and unhappiness, create a space for joy or grief, and can add an extra layer of experience to our everyday lives. The same can be said of anything sensory, that matters to you. Some people are more visual and find visual ways to express themselves.

Even for a profoundly deaf person like me, music can be therapy and a means of releasing emotions, and expressing them. I attended Nordoff Robbins Music Therapy for a short period of time when a teenager, and would always head towards the drums as a way to release pent up frustrations and anxiety. It worked on a level that not much else did, except for creating art or dancing. As much as I loved reading, something so physical with a level of noise and rhythm reached inside and allowed me to immediately express everything I was going through. A certain element of tension and frustration builds up within most deaf children and adults, existing in a hearing world (still) full of barriers of communication and connection. To find spaces to express that in a way that doesn't harm you is crucial.

The film *Lost and Sound*, for example, directed by Lindsey Dryden, is a documentary exploring deaf people's connections to music. It opened up a fascinating dialogue about how human beings, and deaf people in particular, experience music—and notably how it engages the brain. The film had a number of neuroscientists in discussion about how the brain explodes into activity when we listen to or experience music—like a gymnasium for the mind. They made the crucial point that everyone—hearing, deaf—listens to music differently, engaging all the senses, and on the deepest level it is unique for every individual. Though I would have liked to have known what music is like for profoundly deaf people like myself, I have known enough deaf people to see how they all engage with music in their own ways—some via musical hallucinations and earworms, some with vibrations and sound, whilst still others play musical instruments—it feels like there are many ways to connect with our own personal internal rhythms. Life is full of diverse ways to engage and express ourselves, and music is just one of those possible avenues.

Part Two:

Matters Of The Heart

An Ode To Love

To love is hard. It is also easy. It can bathe you in euphoria or dig the knife in hard. Bittersweet, like goodbyes, or soft, like a warm, cocooning blanket. It's the easiness of giving, and the struggle of acceptance. In short, love isn't fixed, immovable: it changes with you, with your circumstances, the struggles you go through. It flows between people, between people and animals, and flows within yourself. Like the energy of the wind, it invisibly surrounds us, though we often feel it as if it is a physical thing.

It takes courage to truly love. Humans forget that to love is to be vulnerable: to expose ourselves, show who we truly are, the dark, the grey and the light. It isn't about perfection, the promise of forever. It means exposure, uncovering: seeing. You see someone and allow yourself to be seen. This is why loving is so hard, and so easy.

It's hard to show yourself to someone. Especially when you've been wounded. When we hurt the ones we love, we do it knowing, yet forgetting, that they they've seen us, and we've seen them, and we will be breaching that trust, the trust where we hold their true selves in our hands. It's fragile, and yet as strong as a constant heartbeat.

To show yourself as you truly are is to pull off the mask of social propriety, to hold a safe space in which people are able to grow, escape to, and feel renewed. To accept each other, to understand each other, we have to be willing to fully see people—their shadows, their grey areas, their light, their darkness. To try to entirely see someone can take years—if not a lifetime.

Sometimes, that seeing is interrupted. You might drift away from someone, only to be reminded of who they truly are again later. Love is the same no matter the social boundaries of your relationship with each other. It is only the intention and the relationship rules that change. The feeling itself remains timeless—something you have that you extend to all those you consider friends, sisters, brothers, human, even other animals. To love is to see, and try to understand.

It is true that actions speak louder than words. Even though I live in words, I know that words are nothing without intent and action. Listening, watching, extending yourself towards others—by giving them your time, your solicited advice, your help, or your ideas—is a symptom of love. To be loving, we have to do. We all have our preferred language of love. For some, it means giving and receiving encouragement. For others, it might be small gifts every now and then, or lending each other things, or sharing. We extend love to strangers by donating or giving our time.

Empathy is a form of love towards other people, even if it doesn't quite feel like it. You stretch yourself, you see people's lives and struggles, you attempt to understand and put yourself in their shoes. You imagine what they have seen, and how they have experienced it. Listening to their stories, being curious and compassionate, is love. We don't always feel enough love in these times of screens and alienation, where loneliness abounds. E.M. Forster's 'Only connect!' is truer now than it has ever been: to connect is important and necessary to solve a multitude of social, psychological, and political issues. To reach out, and to ask, is both scary but necessary for a wholehearted life.

How do we continue to love even through grief and endings? How can it be possible to still retain a part of us that thrives on love when loving, at times, is one of the hardest things we can do? We learn to stretch towards loving ourselves. This kind of love is self-compassion and kindness. So often we talk to ourselves as we would a hated enemy, whipping ourselves with harsh words, saying and believing that we aren't worthy of kindness and attention, of love and respect.

To love ourselves means to forgive the mistakes we make, to learn from them, and to know when we need to look after our inner and outer landscape—to practice self-care, to feed ourselves, to feed our minds and hearts, to do what brings us joy. Loving ourselves—like loving others—can be easy, but most of us find it a struggle, needing to take it day by day, unlearning lies we tell ourselves or that we have been fed. To love ourselves is to understand that we are worthy of the love that other people give us. It is to be our own best friend in times of need, but also knowing when we need to ask for help.

Love is growth. Like a tree that is rooted, reaching for the sky. It encourages us to become the best we can be—to fulfil our potential, grow into our power as compassionate human beings, and to live well, mindful of the effect we have on the world around us. To love others is to also encourage them to reach their fullest potential, to believe they can be their best selves, but also seeing that they are whole, worthy human beings just as they are in this moment.

We see what they want, or we help them to see what their dreams are, and we celebrate with them when they reach milestones. We are also there for the failures, and remind them that failure is part of the learning process, and that all we need to do is get back up and try again, or try it differently. Growth comes from learning the lessons that life teaches us, becoming wiser and full of gratitude.

Of course, the pain that comes with love leaves scars and lessons too. Losing people, or almost losing them, can fundamentally change the way you see the world. We are all survivors in some way, and learning to keep hope—to be hopeful—is not naïve but part of the great adventure of love. Even at the darkest moment, to move towards hope can save your life. Hope is the promise that we can change something, that we can move forwards, that there is something remarkable to live for, and that above all, love can be the guiding light in your life. If something doesn't work, there is still love. For yourself—for your family—for community. To keep on loving in the face of everything we see in the world is resilient and human.

On Being Owned By Cats

What is it about cats that captivates human beings? They are often aloof, mysterious, and contrary. People who live with cats, the saying goes, are not cat owners, but cat owned. I've been 'owned' by cats since I was a baby, and have been lucky enough to get to know six cats so far. I love all kinds of animals, from Aardvarks to Zebras, but cats, of all types, from the most pampered pedigree to the tattiest alley cat, have captured my heart and imagination.

The first cat to be a part of my life was Fulham, so named because he was black and white (and so is the football team's kit). His mother was wild, so Fulham was half wild, allegedly half domesticated. His start in life was in a shed in my Mum's colleagues garden. My aunt Helena, at the time, lived in a house with six other nurses, and they wanted a cat, possibly for mousing. My Mum's colleague Charlie was happy to give them a kitten from the litter. On the night Charlie handed him over to my parents, they phoned Helena, ready to take him to Clapham, but Helena had to let them know that they couldn't take him after all: one of her housemates was allergic. At the time, my parents lived in a one bedroom flat without a garden, not an ideal situation for an unexpected cat, and that night they didn't have any cat food. They were cooking a batch of spaghetti bolognaise, so inevitably Fulham dined like a lion that evening on beef mince in rich tomato sauce (hold the spaghetti). My parents told me all about how he had moments of grave peril, using his nine lives well. His nature was one of contrasts—he did love affection, but could turn on you when he had enough. It took living with him in close quarters to understand what was and wasn't acceptable to him—when he needed space, when he was about to turn on you, and when he wanted to play or be stroked. Living with him was living on the edge, with a cat that you both feared and loved.

If we wanted to get into the kitchen, and Fulham was in the way, there was no guarantee that you wouldn't get your legs savaged by claws. My sister had to be lifted up and over him by my Dad on a few occasions, but Fulham never hurt her in that way, even though at times he appeared intensely jealous of me and my sister's relationship with our Mum. Yet he gradually accepted us both as part of the family, and I even woke one morning to his rough tongue giving my young face a (to him) much needed clean. In those moments, it was best to move as little as possible. When my Mum decided that Sarah and I could do with the experience of knowing cats that weren't so violent, two little kittens, Quentin and Georgina (named by the breeder), came into our lives, disrupting Fulham's iron-clawed hold over his household. He eventually grudgingly accepted these little usurpers, but unfortunately he clipped both of them on one of their ears, so they always both held the marks of his dominance.

Quentin and Georgina, or Tigger and Gigi, as we often affectionately called them, were absolutely beautiful bundles of white and grey fur. They came to us from a lady called Terry, who had a white-furred, longhaired chinchilla pedigree cat called Molly. Terry made a big impression on me—she was glamorous, kind, and talkative, and only one of three older ladies I've met so far that adore cats with a passion. Quentin was a shorthair with wiry fur, striped tail, a pink nose, green eyes, and a sensitive, shy disposition. Georgina, by contrast, was a longhaired flirtatious, gentle, and sociable lady, with the same pink nose and green eyes. Unofficially,

Quentin was my cat, whilst Georgina was Sarah's—but they were attached to all of us. They were truly stunning, loving cats.

In his early and middle-aged years, Quentin was the typical tom, roaming and adventuring, but always coming home. He was a thoughtful and sensitive cat, always sensing when someone needed comfort or company. He would sit with me at the top of the stairs if I was sad, being patient and allowing me to hug him. If we had visitors, he would run and hide until they had gone, unlike Georgina who would sit in the centre of a room and roll over looking beautiful and asking for attention. Georgie was the most huggable and affectionate cat I've met—she loved nothing more than being picked up and held like a baby. However, she was a fierce huntress, bringing in rats and mice and frightening them to death.

Fulham lived to a ripe fourteen years old, but his life ended too soon. At that time, we allowed him to go out of the front and the back gardens, but the front had a road. We live on a hill, so the steep road meant that cars used to (and still occasionally do) speed down. Fulham was a little deaf in his older age, and liked to lie in the middle of the road. I came home one day and found that Fulham had been rushed to the vets, and our Mum had to tell us that he had been in an accident. It was devastating—he had a soft spot in everyone's heart, despite his contrary nature, and I realised how much I loved the little terror. We stopped letting any of our cats out of the front of the house as a result.

Our parents decided to allow Georgina to have one litter of kittens before she was neutered. They made an ill-advised promise to us that we could keep one of the kittens if there was a black and white cat in the litter—probably assuming that because of Georgie's pale colouring, the chances were slim. The same week that Fulham died, Georgie was taken to the vets because Mum had a suspicion that she was pregnant. The vet told her that she was ready to drop: she gave birth to a litter of kittens the Sunday of that week, under the darkness of a bed. It was a bit of a shock when they discovered that all the kittens were white and brown tabbies apart from just one black and white longhaired tuxedo ball of fluff with a black smudge on her nose. We called her Flossie, after one of my childhood books, *Our Cat Flossie*, by Ruth Brown. She had her mother's green eyes and a pink nose.

These three—Quentin, Georgina, and Flossie, lived long, happy lives, with a few mishaps along the way. Like most cats, they had times when they discovered the limits of their nine lives, and moments when they exercised their territorial rights in the garden. I've mentioned that Georgina was a fierce huntress—she was the only one amongst the three that brought in mice or rats, usually alive, to terrorise. On one occasion, there was a loud banging and crashing downstairs: she came running in chasing a mouse. She scrabbled around underneath the cupboard in the hall, whilst Flossie sat behind her wide-eyed, and Quentin, aloof, observed the drama. Another time, whilst my Mum, sister and I were on holiday in New York, my Dad was calling us with updates since Georgina had brought in a rat. Unfortunately, she didn't bother dealing with it, so my Dad was left with the unpleasant task of rat catching.

Quentin had one major mishap when he went missing for a while, but my parents found him in the lane out of the back of the garden, with a broken leg. He was operated on, and his leg healed well because he was young enough to recover. The same leg gave him arthritis later on in life. Quentin's older years were a little more difficult: he had high blood pressure, eventually becoming blind. The vet gave us months with him, but Quentin gave us years instead. It was hard for him at first—he had to adapt to using his sense of smell, his sensitive paws, whiskers, and hearing rather than his sight—but his resilience got him through it, and we gave him plenty of extra attention. He developed a number of adorable quirks during this time. The first was the way he communicated with us—an extremely loud vocal call, and he would have conversations with you if you replied to him. The second was the way he would 'tap' you with his paw—and his claws—in a gentle, but insistent way, often 'chatting' to you at the same time. He would often find his way upstairs to the top of the house, get onto the bed, and call into my face, tapping my nose. I couldn't hear the noise without my hearing aids, but the claws were a little disconcerting first thing in the morning, as was the fishy breath!

Georgina, on the other hand, became incredibly jealous of her brother during this time. It may just have been that he walked into her face at times, and she would smack him on the nose. She didn't quite seem to understand how he had become different. Yet there was no mistaking that the attention we gave to him was upsetting to her, so we tried to make sure she got extra time too. Flossie, rather than let anything faze her, was affectionate with him, often sleeping next to him on a sofa. She would clean his head and face for him. Flossie was a bridge between the two, and was equally as affectionate with her mother. She was by far the most playful of the three, having 'mad hours' every night when she would rush from room to room, with big dilated black pupils, up and down the stairs. Flossie wasn't always as willing as the other two to be held or stroked, but she became much more sociable with her humans towards middle age. Her calling card was affectionate licking and then nipping of fingers. The only time she let me hold her like a baby was in her twilight years, when I was using the laptop. Her favourite thing to do was find the highest place possible to sit, and peer down at us.

When I would come home from university, Quentin would turn his back to me and sulk, rebuking me for having been gone so long. He would eventually soften, but it was difficult to realise how long it must have felt for him. It was always hard to leave them, to miss them. There is no shame in admitting that you're someone who appreciates home, and I certainly do. Home to me may have been difficult sometimes, but it was also a place of acceptance, love, and the cats. I've lived without animals for short stretches of time, and it felt like a part of me was missing. The bond between human and animal is real and though it can't be measured or seen with the eye, it is based on trust and love. I don't consider cats to be children, because they grow and need different things throughout their lifetimes, just as humans do. They are companions, part of the family, but they don't belong to you—you can't own a creature, because they are themselves, a living, breathing thing. You can be a caretaker, which is different to 'owner', and gives you more of a stewardship role. At the same time, animals give us a different perspective on life and living—we will never truly understand what is going on in their minds, but we cross the species divide to mutually care for and love each other.

Living with cats (and animals) also teaches us about life and death, love, and letting go. The biggest heartbreaks have always been the endings, but they also teach us about how we can heal, and love again. Losing all three of them, Quentin when he was nearly 17, Georgina at 18, and Flossie at 16 (a year after Georgina), was always going to be difficult—each bereavement was different. Quentin's death hit me hard, because it was sudden, overnight—he went into heart failure. We had some time to say goodbye to him the day we took him to the vets for his injection, but it was a heavy grief, in the middle of a hot July day. We had to make the decision to treat him with kindness and have him put to sleep; we did the same thing with the girls because they both developed hyperthyroidism in later life, and after they deteriorated, it was eventually time for each of them. It's never easy to judge when the right time is, but cats will let you know in their own ways.

Flossie was the last of our childhood pets to leave us. She scared us a few months before she died—but the relief was immense when we realised that she still had some time left. It was nearing the end of summer 2013, and the sadness settled over the house. It was difficult working from home, without any companion whilst I was writing, and I found myself more than a little heartbroken. A trip to Lancashire to see my Granny's cousin Marjorie was a good break, especially since she had been looking after cats her whole life, and was another glamorous, gentle cat-lady—someone who adores cats with a passion, like Terry did. At the time, she had two cats, Jamie, a ginger Tom, and Sally, a black cat with soulful eyes, and it was wonderful to spend a bit of time with them. At home, the next door neighbour's cat, Bob (so-called for his missing tail), an affectionate three legged tabby, became a welcome distraction, visiting me in the garden and out the front of the house. I missed Flossie waking me up in the mornings and napping with me until I got up. If I saw a cat, they seemed to want to come towards me, perhaps sensing that they could trust me. Or, in that strange sixth sense that animals sometimes have, they sensed that I was a human in need of comfort.

It was in late August, and early September, not long after Flossie's death, that we decided to adopt two young cats from the National Animal Welfare Trust (NAWT) in Watford. It was difficult not to want to adopt all the cats we saw, the way most people feel when visiting shelters, but some of them were single adoptions, and considering we were a house of five adults, we wanted to give two cats a home, at least. We spotted two cats—a brother and sister—online, and decided to visit them. Their names were Gingernut, a shy, unsocialised ginger tabby tom, and Marmalade, a chatty, sociable tortoiseshell lady. At the time, we felt that they had got the names back to front, so we were sure that we would rename Gingernut Marmalade and change Marmalade's name to Chocolat, because she reminded us so strongly of a sassy Parisian lady, a little like Marie, the sassy kitten in the Aristocats. The first time we met her and she was let out of her enclosure, she walked up and down the rows of other cats hissing—exactly like the scene where Thomas O'Malley (the alley cat) teaches the kittens to hiss.

Adopting cats was different to getting to know cats from kittens. The only thing the NAWT staff could tell us about their previous home was that they had been born into a house with too many cats, and hadn't had the socialisation that kittens need to be comfortable and friendly with humans. We could see straight away that Marmalade, the ginger boy, was timid, twitchy, and slow to warm up to new people, but as he settled himself in, he became close to my husband Dan and had a good, but still sometimes uncertain, rapport with me. He went as far as being happy to sit on my lap occasionally, and he was that rare cat that loved belly rubs. His purr was immense, a car engine of a purr, belying the timid little squeak that he used to communicate with us humans. His eyes were liquid gold, and he had little pink jellybean toes. His anxiety with other humans never quite disappeared, though, and his timidity could feel as if you were being rejected, though that was just his nature, and he continued to develop his confidence in a short space of time.

Chocolat, on the other hand, though she took a little while to warm up to us all, was (and is) more than happy to be stroked and fussed over. As so often is the case with tortoiseshell (tortie) cats, she had a lot to say and many different ways in which to say it. This was the biggest surprise—that she constantly wanted to talk to us, express her displeasure and opinion, complain, and tell us what was on her mind. Though I can't always tell, it seems that she has different timbres and volumes of voices for different moods. She often complains about something in the next room, or mews her way up the stairs to find us. In contrast to Marmalade's little squeak, her vocal gymnastics filled (and fill) the house.

They both looked after each other, grooming, play fighting, and sometimes sleeping in the same cat bed. Chocolat could be a little annoyed with her brother, smacking him on the head from time to time, but he absolutely loved her and put up with her slight annoyance. If she was alone, he would decide to curl up with her, and sometimes I would find them cheek to cheek in the sweetest little huddle I've ever seen. We kept them indoors for quite a while after we first adopted them, as the neighbour was doing some building work, and with Marmalade's anxiety, felt it was better to let them out for the first time in calmer circumstances.

When they did first go out, they loved it. They both took to their new territory, and always came home for food and attention. I felt, in the end, that this independence calmed them both down, though Marmalade always kept that edge of timidity and flightiness.

One week in September 2015, Marmalade went missing. It happened overnight. He would usually be in like a shot when breakfast, lunch, or dinner was served (gobbling down his food), and that day, he didn't come in for any of his meals. His sister was confused and kept going into the garden and calling for him. We thought of every possibility—that he may have been shut in somewhere, or that someone else was feeding him, or that he had injured himself, or perhaps roamed too far and couldn't work out his way back. As the week dragged on, and we put up posters, and Dan went on daily walks around the neighbourhood, we started to realise that he may not come home. Chocolat was subdued and came with us when we searched for him in the garden and in the lane behind.

At this point, it took an immense amount of patience, to not fall apart at the seams. It's difficult to explain the attachment humans feel for the animals we share our lives with. I'm not the kind of person who feels that animals are child substitutes—to feel that way would be to do a disservice to them. Rather, they are companions, and we provide shelter, food, and attention when they need it. Since there are many domesticated cats and dogs needing homes in shelters, we have a responsibility to look after them. The latest theory is that cats domesticated themselves, for food, survival, and comfort—how like a cat!—so humans need to be kind, responsible, and caring towards them. In return, they give us affection, and yes, love. I love, and have loved, the cats we have looked after throughout my lifetime so far. So to lose Marmalade, no matter how irrational, felt like I had failed him in some way, even though cats often roam, and it is much more common than I realised for them to go missing.

As the months passed, that uncomfortable, grieving feeling

lodged itself in. When a cat goes missing, it feels like you are constantly waiting. Waiting, holding on, expectant, hoping. Even now, a small part of me is still waiting, even though I have accepted that he may never come home. His sister fills the house with her presence and her voice, and more than makes up for his absence. The little ginger patch above her eye, and the one little ginger toe with a pink pad, reminds us every day of her brother. Ironically, she went missing herself for twenty four hours a couple of years ago, which was terrifying, and found her way home in the middle of the night, just before dawn, starving, both for food and attention. Our theory is that she was shut in somewhere—ever since, I have learned to accept that she will always come back because she loves us, her home, and her garden.

In essence, sharing my life with cats has taught me to love more. It keeps your heart open. When our childhood companions died, I felt as though I couldn't love another animal quite as deeply, but Chocolat has proven me wrong, and shown me that the human heart can heal, and has many rooms for many loves.

Hygge and the Little Things

'Happiness consists more in the small conveniences of pleasures that occur every day, than in great pieces of good fortune that happen but seldom to a man in the course of his life.'

— Benjamin Franklin.

When I was a child, sometimes I would get so bored that I was forced to improvise, to figure out what it was that would bring me the most happiness in that moment. Often, it was re-reading some of my favourite books, or playing with toys, even picking up some paints and pencils. I would become absorbed in the moment, oblivious to anything else. Though I would complain about large family gatherings, wanting nothing more than to curl up in a corner and read, afterwards I would feel that tired but happy glow that comes from being around people who care and know you well. The difficulties—the lack of power when you're a child, the school playground, homework, friendship problems, and early mornings—were cushioned by small joys that made life easier, more comfortable, creating a vibe of acceptance and safety. This is what the ideal of 'home' means—a place you can go to that buffers you and comforts you each day, a place of warmth.

Becoming an adult, I was more conscious of feeling like happiness was seen as a pursuit. It became more about buying products that would make life more comfortable or exciting. Before the world financial crisis of 2008, capitalism, identity, and happiness were, in my mind, bound up together, which made it all the more difficult to maintain a feeling of contentment when I had less income as a student. Consumer culture was in full swing in the nineties and oos, and being a teenager during that time involved pestering your parents for Baby-G watches and Buffalo platform trainers. Eventually, I grew out of this capitalist idea of happiness, and by the time I went to university, I was more interested in reading and experiencing independence. Happiness came in the form of my relationships—friends, family, my now-husband—good food, company, and exploring the world.

Being a poor student meant that I relied more on small everyday pleasures. I couldn't burn candles in our university house, but I adorned my room with garlands of fairy lights and cosy blankets. My own room became a retreat that I escaped to when I wanted some introvert time alone to read, watch Charmed or Lord of the Rings on DVD, and have a cup of tea with some crumpets. Even now, when I've had a difficult time, cosiness is what I seek: bundling up somewhere warm with plenty of blankets, a cup of tea or hot chocolate, and a good film or book. These comforts are truly the best way to soothe yourself when life feels like it's becoming too much.

Although the idea of appreciating and being grateful for the little things in life seems like a particularly new and even middle-class thing, we all find small everyday enjoyments that create a sense of wellbeing and happiness. It varies from person to person—one person's hot chocolate is another person's builder's tea. It's that happiness when you get home after a long day and sink into the couch, put your feet up, and relax. It's meeting with a friend after work and catching up. It's a cosy Sunday with roast dinner in the oven, slowing down. It could even be after a long walk with a friend, sitting down in a cosy pub with a pint. It's these joys that make life what it is, despite the big, amazing events that might occasionally happen to us—like going on a holiday or getting a pay rise. These small habits and occurrences form the background and cushion of a life. Learning to appreciate them, and seek them out, is what makes life less stressful, slower, and more focused in the moment.

It's no coincidence that Hygge (pronounced Hoo-ga), has become so popular. I feel that we all desire a sense of comfort and safety, especially with the devastating social and political problems in the world. It is restorative and elevates the everyday into something special—candles and warm pools of light, small gatherings, comforting food, rusticity, a make-do-with-what-you-have ethic, and a feeling of gratitude. It instils certainty into a world that seems more uncertain than ever. You don't have to be rich to appreciate Hygge—in fact, it eschews wasteful capitalism and focuses more on what you have, and using that to make life comfortable. It works well in winter and autumn, but there are things you can do in spring and summer that work too (lanterns, fairy lights, happy gatherings with good food, film nights, long evenings reading).

Introverts will appreciate that Hygge is about quiet, reflective moments too. Since Danish culture seems (at least from what I've noticed) to enjoy introverted pursuits, such as reading, hiking, smaller, quieter gatherings of friends and family, it seems the ideal kind of cultural zeitgeist that introverts will sagely nod their head to. Hygge is also about building stronger, deeper relationships with fewer people, which is something that introverts prefer. This isn't to say that extroverts won't also love the concept of Hygge, more that introversion and Hygge seem to be a match made in heaven. What better excuse to curl up and read with something hot to drink?

There is a danger that adopting other cultural customs and concepts could be exploitative. The question is whether something truly adds value to our lives, and whether we are just following a trend for something from a different culture. There has been an explosion in the popularity of self-help and philosophy books exploring concepts from other cultures, such as the Japanese Ikigai, Dutch Gezelligheid (similar to Hygge), the Swedish Lagom, and Swedish Fika. Life philosophy, as a rule, is fascinating, and often truly does add value to our lives, and helps us to think differently. For example, Ikigai, in simple terms, is about having a 'reason for being'. In some ways similar to Hygge, it calls for us to appreciate the small and big habits and routines that give our lives meaning. Lagom is the idea of something being 'not too little, but not too much'—the idea of something being 'just right', and again, applies to all kind of things, from lifestyle to how much we work. The popularity of these concepts is nothing new—self-help is a burgeoning and useful category of books that encompasses everything from mental health to life philosophy—and in our increasingly stressful and ever-connected world, learning ways to change our lives and take some control over our happiness could be a good thing.

Mostly, the popularity of Hygge is due to the perception that Danes are some of the happiest people on earth. They consistently score high on global happiness index rankings, no doubt because of a convergence of different factors—but most Danes, according to Meik Wiking in his insightful book *The Little Book of Hygge*, cite Hygge as a major contributor to their contentment and happiness. In the UK, we don't have an overarching cultural concept that underpins everyday life, which we seek to instil in every moment. Regardless, it is also important not to sentimentalise or idealise other cultures, as every country and nation have their own social and political issues. Happiness is different to everybody, and yet perhaps we also need to think about those small joys that we couldn't do without, that elevate our lives above merely existing. We don't need to take on Hygge as if it's a pursuit (which is beside the point), but add aspects of it to our lives, so that each moment becomes warmer and more substantial. Perhaps use some ideas from Ikigai to create meaning in your life, and also make some time for a Swedish-style coffee break with Fika.

I've always loved the sight of a candle dancing, and warm, soft lighting is more beautiful and infinitely more calming than bright, harsh light. Everything that underpins Hygge is important to me, and no doubt are also what most people would agree are fundamental to their happiness. Maybe the trick is to find ways to add more of it. Our modern lives are full of stressful, disconnected moments, and perhaps concepts such as Hygge are the antidote.

Loneliness

How do I know loneliness? I know it well. It comes to me when I want to show someone just how much I understand them, but I can't. It comes to me when I feel misunderstood, apart from someone. It comes when there is a lack of communication, of depth. How do you become comfortable with it? It's the separateness of skin, of one universe contained within an individual, a universe we can only peer into, have small glimpses of. If you're lucky, you get to see more of that universe, and are always trying to express that canopy of infinite stars to others.

The truth is, you can never quite become comfortable with your own loneliness, your own separateness. We're individuals, and the myth of being completely understood is just that, a myth. Nobody has access to your thoughts, your everyday essential self, except you. Some of us are lucky enough to be able to try and express that essential self, our souls, through some kind of art, a profession, even helping other people. Yet the aching discomfort of loneliness can scrape away at you, remind you that you're alone in your own mind.

Part of being an adult is accepting that discomfort, and coming to terms with it. Not to do so would be to give in to it. We try to distract ourselves from the ache by doing, by seeking amusement and society. In the end, though, we are still left with it. It comes in the moments we are physically alone; it comes in the moments when you are surrounded by people. It hits, sudden, when you are happy and joyful. The sweet ache of sadness. The realisation that in the end, we are all alone.

Loneliness, however, is something we need to become friends with. Settle in, look it in the face, stare at it until you finally understand. Yes, we are alone, but we can connect. Yes, we can't share everything, we can't ever truly know the people we love. We can still love. We can still wait for those moments of connection, those moments seeing glimpses of stars underneath the skin.

Collect those stars, see them, and learn them well. Show people your heart, be vulnerable, be brave with exposing little bits of yourself. Don't peel all your skin off and let it all go at once, but slowly try to show the world—through actions, thoughts, art, love—those bits of yourself that long for connection and understanding. Not everyone will understand, or will want to. There will be people who do.

Sometimes, I look loneliness in the face and it blinds me. The sharpness of it stabs at my lungs, and I have to take a breath. In those moments all I have is writing. All I have is my breathing. All I can do is remember—race back through every moment where I have chosen to connect. The biggest, riskiest fear that I have as a writer is to expose too much of myself. It's a dance between choosing to show little bits of myself, to write myself out onto the page, and the fear of showing too much. Loneliness demands that I show as much as I can, because otherwise, I'm holding back from myself, as well as the world. It's a tightrope dance. A taut tension.

This is why it is such a privilege to read the thoughts of others. To see a painting, illustration, installation, or object made by someone else. They are pieces of their heart, yet also not the whole picture. Just little fragments of a universe, of thoughts and dreams. Physical markers of an attempt to connect. A story—theirs, someone else's—given to us in return for a little understanding, empathy, a moment of recognition. Or to spark imagination, ideas, a reaction within us—so perhaps we will pass it on, make something of our own. So it goes. From one universe to another.

My fear is that we will forget how to be alone, how to bear the loneliness that strikes no matter where we are. In our pursuit for connection, we spend too much time listening to clamour, to hundreds of voices, overwhelming ourselves with the pain and fear of others. So when we return to ourselves, when we look inside and feel that separateness, we can't bear it. It's one of the best things you can do for yourself—sit still, listen to yourself, be present, bear the loneliness, if it comes, so you understand it a little better. So much of life is learning to be emotionally resilient and living with pain. Connect—but connect with your inner life too. Look into yourself and sit with your dreams. Resist the need to be on, doing, all the time. Noise and movement is wonderful, but so is silence and stillness.

This is the same as realising that we are not our emotions. We are not our loneliness, and loneliness is not us. It is a state of mind, a feeling that is temporary. It's there, just as fear is, but it doesn't have to consume us. It can be a companion, but not in the driving seat. It might be a little crowded back there in the backseat, with fear, anxiety, and loneliness, but you have control of the wheel and where you go next. This is how I try to visualise it, every time I write, or speak: I don't have to expose every part of myself, but I can share what I need to share. I can show people little parts of me without giving in to fear. I can quench loneliness, sometimes, by connecting with others and myself.

This is the way I do it—by putting down words, one after another. As Margaret Atwood wrote, in her poem *Spelling*, 'a word after a word after a word is power'. Sending those words into the world is an attempt at saying 'this is a little bit of myself', and each time pushing against the fear of exposure, being braver each time. Writing is risk, but it's also a guard against loneliness. Anything that feels scary, whether writing, making art, sharing a bit of yourself in person or online, is a guard against loneliness. A shout out from one universe into another.

The Imaginative Leap of Empathy

The curse of being a deeply empathic human being is that it's easy to constantly be 'on' and feeling all the time. Watching the news can be torture: the familiar feeling of wanting to help and solve the entire world's problems, but being unable to, leaves you feeling inadequate and more than a little heartbroken. How do you stand in the middle in a place that allows you to care, and be educated about current issues, whilst not sliding into a space of disaffected apathy and cynicism? Since empathy is inherently different to sympathy—empathy is an imaginative leap of feeling and, or thought into another person's shoes, literally feeling, or attempting to feel, their feelings and thinking about their point of view and way of life. Conversely, sympathy is more about pity, feelings of sadness for someone going through a difficult experience. There is a time and place for both, but most people don't want to be 'felt sorry for', which is why empathy is such an important, wonderful tool for human connection.

Cynicism, the little brother of apathy, is easy to slide into and difficult to climb out of. Yet it is possible. The sense that nothing will ever change, that there is no point in trying to make the world a better place, that it will keep on turning, with war, famine, poverty, capitalism, and hate always present. It is the ultimate 'whatever' shrug. The biggest lie of cynicism is that it tells us there is no hope, so we should just carry on living our lives without any moral or social responsibility. It can also lead to a complete eclipse of any kind of feeling or connection with the world at large, leading to a wholesale apathy—a lack of empathy, or even sympathy.

Why do we need empathy? What is so important about it? You'd be forgiven for thinking that with all the moral-panic about the 'age of distraction' and the 'age of narcissism', that people are too self-involved to even try and empathise with other people. Yet I've seen instances of empathy and connectedness through networks of activists, charity workers, creatives, young people, and even within politics. You might even say that just because I've seen it doesn't make it true. This is also true—that just because we see something, just because we've experienced it, doesn't mean that it's the same everywhere. There is always a balance—between light and dark, cynicism and enthusiasm, apathy and empathy. We live in a world of opposites, with all the shades of emotion and states of being in between those opposites. Inside us all, the same opposites and contradictions exist. Just as we have the capacity for boundless compassion, we also have the possibility of boundless cruelty. It is what we choose to do, say, and be, the way we express ourselves, that makes us who we are.

Empathy is what allows us to stretch beyond ourselves into a place of imagination and humanity. It forges connections that have the capacity to create change—whether that is just for one person or a whole community. Instead of a patronising view of charity as pity, we leap and we learn to understand people who are often completely different to ourselves, using that understanding to guide our actions, or asking people what they need. Empathy isn't just about understanding 'good' people, though. It's about understanding the reasons behind people's behaviour and seeing people, seeing them for who and what they are. Sometimes this means understanding people who commit terrible crimes, even as we condemn their behaviour. This is how writers leap into the minds and motivations of their antagonists, and how some of the best fictional villains are the ones we can empathise with, however fleetingly, despite the evil acts they commit. We all share common humanity, no matter who we are or where we come from. Empathy is the recognition of this— the understanding that I am no better or worse than you, and that we are both human beings, living in this moment in time, though our lives may be starkly different.

On a personal level, empathy can change the way we relate to others, yet it also has immense power to change the world through creating positive social and political action. Though we are confronted with many different social issues day to day—from war and gun-control, to online harassment and social movements such as Black Lives Matter—we have the power to learn about and understand social issues more deeply, to listen to how they are affecting people's lives, and what actions we can take informed by this deeper understanding. Being an ally and an empathic human being begins by listening and asking questions, by taking the initiative to forge connections with others. It is possible to become involved in social and political movements when we understand what needs to change—and empathy is often the spark and trigger for that change.

In this time of the decline (and in some places, radical backslide) of social and political progress, a swing towards fundamentalism worldwide, and the deepening chasm between the richest and poorest in the world, empathy and compassion are more important than ever. It isn't just about kindness. Empathy goes beyond and becomes something rebellious, transgressive, something that can make impact far beyond 'acts of kindness'. Social and political change also requires us to understand the views and perspectives of people who are on 'the other side' of our own views, beliefs, and perspectives. In this way, we can find commonalities, and ground that we may be able to work on together. It's a sad fact that most online political discussions are rarely fruitful because we are not truly listening to the other person's point of view. We are listening with a view to respond, rather than with a view to understand. True listening requires us to forget about our own point of view for a while, and to learn all we can about the other person.

In his book *Empathy: A Handbook for Revolution*, Roman Krznaric writes that in the 21st century, we need a radical empathic revolution. I first came across his writing on empathy in *The Wonderbox*. I felt that I wanted to know and understand more about it, and his book *Empathy* delves right in to the various ways we can exercise our own capacity for it, and how it can be a force for change. The more we understand how to use it, and the myriad ways in which it can change the world for the better, the more hope I have for a world that seems, sometimes, to be full of disaster. He outlines six ways in which we can use empathy—cultivating curiosity about strangers, challenging prejudices and discovering commonalities, 'trying' another person's life, listening hard and opening up, inspiring mass action and social change, and developing an ambitious imagination. The six tenets of developing our empathic muscles have great potential to transform our lives.

The six habits of empathy, according to Roman Krznaric, are:

1. Switching on your empathic brain, by asking questions about how we can become more empathic and less self-centred.

2. Making the imaginative leap (by putting yourself in someone else's shoes, trying to put yourself in the shoes of people you have trouble empathising with).

3. Seeking experiential adventures—thinking up a way of immersing yourself in another way of life, whether by exploring another culture (in a non-invasive, sensitive way), or socio-economic background.

4. Practising the craft of conversation—by learning how to truly listen to someone, asking questions about their lives and initiating difficult but necessary conversations (such

as thinking of new ways to talk to someone who you find it hard to talk to).

5. Travelling in your armchair by reading books about cultures and societies you know little about, and watching films and documentaries about people and places different to you.

6. Inspiring a revolution by using empathy to rally people to a social or political cause you care about, and finding ways to use empathy to deepen your understanding about and connection with the natural world.

7. And finally: thinking about which of these habits you would like to develop further, taking steps to do so.

There have recently been some arguments against emotional empathy—the act of feeling what other people are feeling. The arguments essentially posit that emotional empathy becomes more about what you are feeling, about the suffering of others staying within you and leading to burnout. For example, Paul Bloom's essay (and his recent book, also titled *Against Empathy*) in the Boston Review, *Against Empathy*, explains why emotional empathy is all well and good when used in relation to individuals, but more of a hindrance when thinking about how to use policy, activism, and social change to improve the lives of groups of people, and large populations.

The core of his argument is that in general, emotional empathy doesn't necessarily mean that you are a compassionate, caring individual—empathy may instead be an involuntary response, something that we feel, and have no control over. In this way, it doesn't relate to being a moral person, someone who will act to make changes or support causes they feel strongly about. Bloom himself makes the distinction between emotional empathy and cognitive empathy, empathy founded more upon focused, mainly unemotional thinking. This is the type most used by people in social and political policy-making, in activist movements, in psychology, and organisations dedicated to social change.

However, the best way to use empathy, in my own trial and error, is to understand that both types of empathy can be harnessed in different situations. Emotional empathy is to be expected—we feel this when we see situations that upset us, listen to people's stories of hardship, and read books that take us on an emotional journey. The trick is to allow for that, and yet control how we behave, not redirecting the focus on to us, away from the person or people who are suffering. Compassion and thoughtful interactions with other people, pragmatic and practical advice (if sought after), and ways to express that empathy without making it about you is the best possible way to act on emotional empathy. If you're sensitive and susceptible to burning out on feeling the pain of other people, it is important to understand that aspect of yourself and to find ways of constructively taking action, and how to protect your sense of wellbeing.

Empathy, compassion, and imaginative leaps are essential for understanding the lives of those around us and for leading to revolutions—big and small. There is a balance to be found, to guard against burnout and loss of hope. At its best, empathy has the possibility to change the world for the better when used and harnessed with intelligence and courage.

Why Jane?: A Truth Universally Acknowledged

In 1995, the BBC aired the iconic series of *Pride and Prejudice*, directed by Andrew Davies (of later Dr Who revival fame). I was in my last year of primary school, approaching age 11. I was hooked—although I couldn't quite tell you why—during my viewing of the series, I was so desperate to know what happened next that I decided to read the book.

I was already a major bookworm, devouring worlds, characters, and stories with all the gusto of someone whose life depends upon it. My parents read to me and my sister when we were young: I was lucky enough to have parents who nurtured my love for words and stories, got me a library card, and would buy me books when they could. I felt as at home in the dusty library stacks, as I did in the new-page promise of bookshops. My favourite books were already falling apart, with bits of chocolate in the seams and dog-eared pages where I had marked my place.

With *Pride and Prejudice*, there was a turning point. It was the hardest book in terms of language that I had read thus far, but I persevered, was rewarded, and immediately fell in love with the works of Jane Austen. At that age, it was the fantasy element of romance, but also the fiery, witty repartee of Elizabeth Bennet that enraptured me. She wasn't afraid to speak her mind: and though her prejudice and assumptions led her to make some fatal judgements, it balanced the pride of Darcy, who was less the perfect hero than someone who eventually (like most of us, I suspect) fell for the wit and sparkling eyes of Elizabeth.

In later years, with the vogue for screening and filming adaptations of Jane Austen's works—*Persuasion, Sense and Sensibility, Emma, Mansfield Park*—I read most of her novels. Each of them has something to offer the reader, and the subtle wittiness and wisdom that, with the passing years, I have begun to appreciate more. They are novels of Jane's time—they speak of the flirtation games and courtship rituals that men and women played—yet they are also extremely contemporary and stand the test of time. I have never been able to quite sink into a Charles Dickens novel as I can with an Austen.

Part of the appeal of the novels is that the women at the centre of them are strong, yet fallible and vulnerable. They all learn something about the nature of life and love, character and humanity. Elizabeth, the most well-known of Austen's heroines, is an intelligent, bold young woman, who—as we might say nowadays, takes no shit. As I mentioned earlier, her fatal flaw is that she can be prejudiced, without knowing all the facts of a story, and can assume the worst of someone's character. This is something that we can all relate to; precisely because it is such a believable predicament to find yourself in, we sympathise with her.

Emma, again, is a strong, vivacious, opinionated young woman, who delights in matchmaking her friends. Intent on making the best possible matches for them, she miscalculates, landing herself in hot water and making a number of heart-breaking mistakes which she has to put right. Emma has a big heart: her matches come from a place of good intentions. She can be thoughtless and lacks skills of fine observation, a hard lesson to learn and to correct. By the end of the novel, however, she has understood that her talents don't lie in matchmaking, and has tried to set her mistakes right, as well as, naturally for the main characters of an Austen novel, finding her own match, who was right in front of her the whole time.

Persuasion, however, is a novel I have come to appreciate more since first reading it. It is all about second chances; how we make mistakes, recognise them, and grow from them. The themes within the novel are the most mature of all Austen's works, and though not as polished as some of her earlier books, is still a wonderfully warm, thoughtful, and intelligent novel. As I have come to understand the need for second chances, the more I have understood the emotional courage of Anne Elliot and Captain Wentworth. The lessons from this novel are interesting—how we need to trust our own feelings and intuition, and have the courage of our convictions, rather than trusting the dubious wisdom of people who may not have our best interests at heart. Only you know what is right for you.

Jane Austen's writing is deceptively light and airy, yet delves into the domestic and social concerns of her time. By focusing on the lives of women, she cast a light upon the private realm of domesticity. In *Pride and Prejudice*, for example, Elizabeth and her sisters are in a precarious position because their father's estate will not be entailed to either them or their mother on the event of his death; instead, the odious Mr Collins, an extended relation, will have ownership. Though not uncommon for the time, it meant that finding a husband for Elizabeth and her sisters was presented as a background pressure, always there, always hanging over them.

Elizabeth wants to marry for love: a luxury when her only hope of economic survival is to marry well (in this case, someone who was of comfortable means, at the very least). Elizabeth's stubborn determination to marry someone she loves, or at least deeply likes, means that she turns down Mr Collin's romantic overtures, thus not assuring her sisters or mother economic stability. Happily, both Jane and Elizabeth marry for love, but perhaps Mrs Bennet's 'nerves' are a little more understandable, even though she isn't exactly someone with much good sense. The reality was that many women may have accepted the first man to offer, whether or not they had a happy, loving marriage.

Laurie Penny, in her book of essays *Bitch Doctrine*, writes about how Austen's novels can be read as horror stories. Horror stories, because the heroines are all trapped in a cage of patriarchal culture—facing poverty, loss of reputation, and social isolation. Jane Austen never married herself—she had a potential brush with marriage at the beginning of her writing career—and as Penny writes, the novels are stories of how women survive in the cages culture and society have built for them. Under this lens, the novels are fascinating because as women trying to survive for different reasons (at least in UK culture), in a different time period, we can't help but root for these women to thrive. If Elizabeth Bennet is stubborn enough to stick to her desire to marry for love, it counts as a kind of resistance, even though marriage might come with its own rules and strictures. At least she values her own happiness, her own security—and by some particular twist of luck, she manages to ensure the security of the rest of her family too.

With Emma, too, there are clashes between Emma's understanding of class, and good matches, and what she wishes could be true. When she tries to set up Harriet Smith (a young woman without 'title' or known parentage) with Mr Elton, the local vicar, without any sensitivity to Harriet's attachment to Robert Martin, a local farmer, and Mr Knightley rebukes her for it, we can see that Emma's fantasies, the way in which she copes with a lack of purpose in her life, clash with the reality of a rigid class system, where people of different classes rarely marry or mix. Her treatment of some of the poorer people she mixes with also betray her classist opinions, despite her meddling in their love lives and marriage prospects. At the same time, as the novel progresses, the ambivalence of Austen's treatment of class shows that there are just as many questions still unanswered—the class system is still turning, still rigid, and Harriet marries Robert after all, the man she was set to be engaged to before Emma's attempts to match-make.

You could say that Jane Austen's novels cleared the path for women to write more about the daily lives, loves, and adventures of women. If Jane hadn't written, I doubt my life would have taken the path it has: reading *Pride and Prejudice*, my first fully adult novel, was a gateway into my appreciation of writing. Her heroines are enduring, passionate—even the quietest, in the end, find a way towards the lives they want. Of course, in regency England, that meant a good man as a husband, but even if we ignore that aspect, they are still wholly themselves. Unlike Shakespeare's Katharina, in *The Taming of the Shrew* (where she is submitted to brainwashing and cruelty), Elizabeth is still herself—witty, opinionated, and head-strong—and Mr Darcy loves her for it. Along with the Brontës, Jane Austen deserves her place in great literature.

Teaching Myself To Let Go

Letting go is an art in itself. It doesn't come naturally to me. I'm one of those people who will analyse something to death – will take hold of a slight, or a perceived slight, or a worry, and will dig deeper and deeper, sometimes to come up with a kernel of truth, or just having the soil bury me under. I've had a number of life events that everyone experiences—loss of friendship, loss of community, loss of a sense of self, and the physical loss of people through death. The heart stubbornly holds on, desperate to understand.

All loss feels equal, no matter how it happens. Logically, I understand that losing friendships along the way in life is often a natural thing. People change, or move away, or you change and let the friendship go, or some friendships don't survive past certain time periods—childhood, school, university, moving jobs, moving away from a community (physically or emotionally). Yet it is always difficult to accept these transitions. Some friendships are tinged with a sense of nostalgia—for a time when you were different, when life may have been easier. In reality, the passage of time shapes you. Ideally, you are wiser, have more experience, and a better understanding of life and love. When I think back, I can remember the struggles I had, as well as the moments of happiness. The way some friendships end also leave a lot to be desired, and some of those old hurts sting, even given that you have moved on with your life.

It's not easy to admit that the end of friendship is one of the hardest losses to cope with. Your friends are your chosen family: people you have bonded with and trust. As a wise person once told me—people come in and out of our lives, sometimes just for a short time, and sometimes for longer—often for a purpose. To be able to let go of friendships requires an understanding of how they have enriched your life, and changed you. Even the ones that end badly, in some ways teach you big lessons, like how to treat people well, and how to be graceful. Perhaps the hardest thing is to keep our hearts and minds open to new friendship, despite the pains of losing old ones. You lose a part of your history with the end of a friendship—the trick is to try and see it as a new beginning.

Beginning again is a theme that threads through my life. I've written before about how every new day presents possibility, even though we are in many ways the same person, with the same habits as yesterday. Every new day is a chance to start anew, and to let go of the hurts and struggles you experienced yesterday. For me, this is a work in progress. It is always an ongoing process, with no real end in sight. Every time I start a new writing or creative project, I am letting go of the work I have done in the past. Once I finish something, and send it out into the world, it no longer belongs completely to me. When you let go of what you have achieved, you learn to move forward to the next challenge. Everything you do teaches you something new. For example, when I began work on this book, I was a different person to the one I am now. It's likely that once I've finished this book and send it out into the world, I'll be a different person in some way again. I'll follow that person towards writing something different. What I wrote six years ago is different to what I write now. The more you do, the more you learn, the more you change and understand how to let go.

That thread weaves itself through my relationship with my husband too. We have both had to let go of past hurts and difficulties. Every relationship requires people to learn to release the pains of the past and move towards the future together. To grow together, towards each other, rather than away from each other. Doing the work of often complicated emotional support and understanding, even when you're struggling yourself. Being brave enough to know, and hope, that you will survive even when you hit rocky terrain. It often feels as if hope and being able to let go of the past are linked together. Hope is different to blind optimism—hope pulls you through gently, a torch in the darkness.

Even when death parts you from your loved ones, or people you once knew; even beloved family pets. Love is a wild thing, irrepressible, and when a connection is severed, you are still left with that love. Experiencing loss in death is different for everyone. There is no linear, direct way of letting go. Our minds will play tricks, and our hearts will be trickier. Still, as time flows on, breathing room enters your grief, a slow, gentle space that allows you to let go of the pain. The sharpness is slackened, allowing for a softness; allowing you to remember with happiness, as well as sadness.

Eventually, that space will widen, becoming a vast field. At first, you don't want to let go, fearing that you will forget. That the memories will fade. Some do, but others often become sharper and clearer, more substantial. Less of a photograph, and more of a film—triggered by the world around you—a certain scent, a sound, a place, a saying. You come to accept that letting go doesn't mean forgetting, or loving any less. It just means a release of pain and fear. An acceptance of how transitory life is, and that it is all the more beautiful for being so.

Losing yourself is trickier. Loss of self can be triggered by anything—from depression to losing or changing career, to losing community. It can be down to losing your sense of purpose, or losing touch with what matters to you. You feel that you don't know quite what you believe, what you think—and what you want. A more extreme loss of self could occur when people lose their memories, suffer dementia, or experience amnesia. We define ourselves in different ways, according to culture, family, peer group, and world-view. By what we enjoy doing, and what we don't enjoy doing. By what we've experienced, and what we would like to experience. It all comes together to form the basis of 'us'. Losing your compass, your passion, meaning, or purpose—could lead towards pain or towards discovery.

Constant rediscovery is how we adapt. Changing roles and life circumstances call for us to let go of who we once were and embrace the unknown. It's been my experience that people don't want to confront the unknown—that often it feels too painful, and too scary. We like our comfort zones, staying within the places we feel safe. Yet I think there is a lot of growth and beauty to be found leaning towards discovering what you don't yet know about yourself, towards changing yourself. You can't always change the circumstances you find yourself in, so changing who you are, what you do, and how you behave allow you to find meaning and purpose. Finding meaning within painful circumstances is often an internal thing. It may not be detectable to the naked eye, and yet inside we are metamorphosing, thinking differently, and learning powerful life lessons.

For example, my parents were devastated when they were given the news that both of their daughters had been diagnosed as deaf. At first, they didn't know what to do, or where to turn. There is a natural grieving process that parents go through when their child has been diagnosed. They are given information and don't know what to do with it. Over time though, they can see how adaptable and resilient their child or children are. My parents, in particular my Mum, had to fight for us to have access across the board—education, social life, entertainment, and within the family. Eventually, she found her passion with becoming a theatre captioner—something that came from the way we had been challenged as a family, by the way she had been challenged to change her life. Life throws us right into circumstances without us feeling equipped for them, and sometimes it is up to us to find a way through, to make connections and forge a new path for ourselves.

In this way, letting go is the wisest and most compassionate action we can do for ourselves. It gives you the courage to discover more about yourself, the world around you, and the people in your life. It unburdens you and yet helps you to learn how better to carry your experiences and responsibilities. It can give you the breath you need when you can't breathe.

Heal

To bend and change is part of life. Yet there are times when we shatter, and we have to put the pieces back together again. There can be pieces missing, or pieces that look different, and we might have to spend time getting to know those pieces of ourselves. The Japanese concept of wabi-sabi, embodied by broken pottery repaired with gold and silver dust mixed with lacquer, is the perfect way to understand and accept that with every mistake and imperfection, every sadness and loss, there is a chance to grow and learn. Imperfection is beautiful and a necessary aspect of human nature. Perfection is impossible. What should we strive towards instead? A greater understanding of and the growth of ourselves and the people around us is rooted in accepting imperfection, even celebrating it.

Healing is different for everyone. To me, it means going back to basics. I pay attention to food, rest, bodily hygiene and movement, giving myself space and the permission to just be, reading an undemanding book, and spending some time outside in nature. Another effective strategy is to do something with my hands— whether DIY around the house or outside, painting, drawing, or colouring, writing by hand, or cross-stitching and embroidery. Gardening works too—potting plants, weeding, clearing old undergrowth, or planting. This can apply to a kitchen garden or indoor plants too, anything that needs to be done by hand. It doesn't matter if you're good or bad at what you're doing—working with your hands or doing physical work is a good way to create motion and movement in your life.

In 2016, a difficult year for many reasons, I made a snap decision to paint my Mum's study, which sorely needed a fresh new look. Doing something for her made me feel good, and conversely made her happy. I didn't stop there. That year saw the landscaping of the garden, the studio cabin built, and plenty of furniture painting, DIY, and physical work. This stopped me from falling apart completely, from losing my way. Work on a project that gives you or someone you love some joy, that involves a sense of moving forwards through time, where you can see the progress you're making.

Of course, when you're lifting out of depression, you have to be gentler with yourself. You do what you can to keep going, to survive and live. I read a wonderful book a few years ago, *Sunbathing in the Rain*, by a poet, Gwyneth Lewis, who wrote about how to heal and look after yourself when within and healing from depression. Everyone experiences depression differently—we have unique memories, experiences, and lifestyles. Not everyone finds the same coping strategies effective when living with it. Gwyneth Lewis's book changed the way I understood my own periods of depression, and how I saw the healing process. Her definition of the opposite of depression—not happiness, as some people tend to mistakenly believe—but feeling alive, matches my own definition of depression as apathy—as not feeling, everything seen and felt through a veil.

So, healing after depression involves allowing yourself to feel. To feel everything, and not shy away from it—accepting feelings and slowly coming alive. Coming out of depression is like waking up from a winter hibernation and being amazed by the way you're bursting into life again—the colour, the green, the possibility of spring. The expansiveness of life returns. You feel more passion for what you love doing. In a particularly difficult bout of depression, when I also grieving for the loss of a relative, reading brought me back to life again, forcing me to feel and empathise with the characters, to feel the full gamut of emotions. Eventually, I was grateful for this, even though it was uncomfortable after having shut down my feelings. When you're prone to depression, you have to learn to develop tools to help you cope during these times—a toolbox—of people you can rely on to help, small actions you can do, that don't feel like too much, self-care strategies, and different activities that take varying amounts of energy for days when you can't do much. Some days, you can barely get out of bed, and having a shower feels like a major achievement. You're allowed to feel good that you managed to do that. In these times, don't overload yourself or take on too much, though if healthy distractions help, then by all means, do what works for you.

Healing isn't always a clean and easy process, though. We're human—we're going to slip into habits that don't serve us well, that don't work in the long run. For me, this is spending days in pyjamas, binge watching Netflix series, alternating between spending time in bed and on the sofa. The 'great unwashed' describes this perfectly. Occasionally, we need to do things like this, to indulge in what is perceived as 'laziness'. We might eat too much junk and don't have the energy to cook. This is why having a tool-kit helps when you're struggling. A tool kit is also about managing your emotions and habits, to help with the overwhelming sense of not knowing what to do. A little bit like a game-plan, it's your personal blueprint for how to look after yourself. It's worth spending a bit of time putting this together for yourself—a list of contacts, a few helpful books, websites that help, things to watch and read to distract yourself (or easy hobbies), places to go, things to do, and basic things that make you feel good. You can also write down the strategies that have helped you in the past, to remind yourself that you have come through before, and it's entirely possible to survive what you're going through now.

Resilience is one of the most important qualities we can have. It doesn't come from ignoring your feelings or swallowing them until you break apart. Resilience is elasticity, is bounce—drawing on your strength to recover from challenges in life—from health issues to emotionally turbulent moments. It doesn't mean never leaning on people or never asking them for help. Sharing means that you feel lighter and hopefully more supported. Building a reservoir of strength isn't easy for anyone, especially when we face challenges that seem they could shatter us to pieces.

The way we think about our emotions and vulnerabilities is an important aspect of learning resilience. Pain and suffering are an inevitable part of life. To understand that we are all going to experience a number of setbacks and challenging events in our lives, and that we can either learn from them and grow, or never recover and fall into despair, is part of the mindset that helps people cope with what they are going through. Every challenge, every difficult time I have been through, has helped me become a little wiser, or has helped me understand myself and other people better. I've learnt more about the nature of what it means to live. There have been moments when I've come close to falling apart, but allowing yourself to feel and acknowledging those feelings is an important aspect of moving forwards.

Gratitude and contentment are good partners to resilience, in that they allow us to be grateful for what we do have in any given moment of our lives. Rather than a focus on the material (although there are some very important material things in everyone's lives), I try to focus on gratitude for friendship, family, nature, experiences, skills, knowledge, and ideas. Contentment can flow from that gratitude—rather than trying to sustain feelings of excitement or joy, contentment is a sustained sense that you have enough, right here in this moment. So much of the world is in a race for more, creating feelings of dissatisfaction and discontent. It takes practice to gain contentment and gratitude, against this ingrained sense of constantly wanting more in terms of material attainment.

In Laura Jane William's kind, joyful and wise book, *Ice Cream for Breakfast*, she writes about how she learnt from the children she looked after that we can, and should, make things in our life an occasion, and that we are allowed to indulge our inner child-like tendencies (not child-ish, child-like). For example, create rituals that make you feel good—a tea for one ceremony, where you use your favourite teapot each day to take a bit of time out, to celebrate just because—or wear that dapper 'special' tie or floaty dress, because it makes you feel amazing. Try not to save things for special occasions, because you are worth it now. Dance around to your favourite music, allow yourself to let go more often. Our adult lives are full of unspoken 'rules' and sometimes those rules strangle us, making us believe we have little control over our own contentment and joy.

Whilst the actions we take give us a certain amount of control over what happens in our lives, that isn't to say that there aren't situations and structures outside of our control. Issues such as sexism, racism, xenophobia, homophobia, ableism, and classism can be difficult to cope with. This is when community and communication help us to weather challenges. People you trust are important when facing difficulties, and it is stronger to ask for help rather than coping with situations alone. It takes courage to reach out when we are at our most vulnerable—but resilience is learning when to be vulnerable and share that with others. To willingly show our vulnerability to others is courageous, especially when we are not sure if that will be accepted or not. Learning our emotional and mental boundaries, too, can help us to know what we are comfortable sharing, and with whom.

Celebrating sharing our vulnerability is part of accepting imperfection. If you live with anyone else for any length of time, we know that they are imperfect, and have habits and quirks we have learnt to live with. Conversely, going through different challenges in life means we become aware of our imperfect reactions and traits. The self is a constantly growing and changing thing. The challenges

I have gone through have changed aspects of my personality, and have given me a greater self-awareness. Wabi-sabi, according to Leonard Koren (the author of the book *Wabi-Sabi: For Artists, Designers, Poets and Philosophers*), defines it as: 'the beauty of things imperfect, impermanent, and incomplete, the antithesis of our classical Western notion of beauty as something perfect, enduring, and monumental.'

The most difficult truth to accept is that we are not here indefinitely. The people we love are not going to be around forever. There is an impermanence to life, a sadness at the core of being human that we have to accept. In Western society, death and decay, imperfection, are rarely addressed in any kind of depth, and sometimes to heal ourselves, we have to accept these truths.

Acknowledging the impermanence of life means that we can then understand that every day counts, that being alive is something precious—every single day is a chance to learn something new. Taking the time to appreciate the circular nature of life—from birth to death—leads to a more balanced approach to living. Humans are imperfect beings, constantly experiencing, suffering, learning, and growing. To heal, accepting that life is in constant flux will help us to become more resilient.

Part Three:
Thinking and Dreaming

For The Thinkers

Being a thinker is not easy in a world that is increasingly hostile towards logical, intellectual, and complex ideas. If you value learning the different sides of a situation or researching into a topic over tribalism and black and white thinking, you might be feeling like the odd one out. When this world of ours is driven by the biased, increasingly politically polarised media we consume, where do you go, and who do you ask when you need to know something closer to the truth?

If you're a thinker, yes, you might be prone to rumination, and over-analysis, but the world needs more people who are less prone to leaping without thinking. Not everything needs to be analysed and critiqued, but there is nothing better, in my opinion, than a deep conversation with a friend putting the universe to rights over a cup of tea or cocktail.

People who think before they leap, debate the pros and cons, or seem led by logical thinking, may at first appear to lack an understanding of emotion, but in my experience, the world would be a much less interesting place without them. Of course thinkers don't lack emotion; they are just led towards a deeper consideration of the world around them. Unchecked emotion can lead us towards calamity; without an understanding of why we react the way we do, a lack of self-awareness, we risk losing perspective.

Thinking clearly comes with practice, and thinking clearly

without judging ourselves takes time. Thoughts are electrical impulses in the brain: they come and go, creating pathways of well-trodden ground. As such, they can be ignored, thought-through, or acted upon. We have a certain amount of power to observe our thoughts and change those that no longer serve us, through a variety of ways—from meditation, to counselling, modern medicine, self-help, or journaling.

Being able to observe, to try to understand something before you commit or become involved in it, can be both an asset and a barrier. On one hand, observation allows you to see all the moving parts, to feel comfortable with a situation, or also help other people understand something more deeply. Yet, we also risk becoming too detached, setting ourselves apart, becoming too reliant on observing as a way of making ourselves comfortable at the expense of others. Seeing observation as a powerful tool is useful, but it still requires balance.

The best kind of thinking is that which doesn't rely too much on the ego, on our need to be right. Being open minded, being able to change our minds, to admit that we don't have all the information— in short, being open to seeing the world from different perspectives—means we are always receptive to learning throughout our lives. The real trick is to understand that learning doesn't stop once we finish school. Learning is out there—in the big wide world, in experience, in a deep commitment to constant reading, exposure to what interests us, or subjects we want to know more about. Never assume you know everything there is to know, or that you've seen all there is to be seen. I feel as if true wisdom comes from accepting we don't, and can't, know everything.

The more I have read, the more I have come to understand this. I will die without having read all that I want to read. I know that there is no point in reading books that I don't enjoy if there is finite time to read and learn. The literature of the world is immense. You find your own path through it, through what interests you, and matters to you most. Everyone reads differently, and what will interest one person, won't interest someone else. Still, there is value to be found in seeking out a variety of different perspectives, rather than just sticking to what you know you will enjoy.

I've found my interests have varied over the years—it has taken me on travels through neuroscience, feminism, popular psychology, memoirs, and history. I've read horror, science fiction, 'literary' fiction, crime fiction, paranormal fantasy, traditional fantasy, romance, slipstream, and steampunk fiction. What this has taught me is that my passion lies in knowledge and imagination, and that books can change your heart and mind. They can be dangerous, and they can be powerful. Sometimes, they raise our consciousness— open our eyes. Well informed people can change the world (and their lives), whether through everyday acts or something bigger.

We need thinkers in this world of ours, just as we need dreamers, pragmatists, doers, and people who are kind and loving. So much of what is around us is the result of people who invented, thought hard about what would make life better, thought about what democracy looks like, thought about how we want to live. Philosophers, inventors, politicians, teachers, writers, activists, leaders. We owe so much to them, and we can follow in their footsteps by learning more about them and what inspired them. To remember that ideas have the power to change the course of our lives. People are still fighting for these big ideas—equality, liberation, love, freedom, peace. These ideas underpin our everyday lives, whether we are aware of them or not. People who make us aware of them are people unafraid of the power of ideas, who know that it can take just one idea to change the course of history.

Often, thinking takes time. It can take years for the seed of an idea to fully develop into a tree of knowledge. Perhaps because our world is so fast, information is cheaper, and easier to get to, and ideas are fleeting, here one moment and gone the next. Yet knowledge and wisdom born of depth and experience are priceless. It takes time to understand more about life, time that we don't think we have. Too much of our time is spent chasing novelty and we become hooked on the rush of immediate gratification. If we are to find answers or to find the right questions to ask, we need to slow down, become patient, take the time to think, sit with ourselves, and become comfortable with our minds. Spend time with writing, with reading, with talking (and listening) to others about a variety of subjects. Become interested and curious in what that you take for granted. Allow yourself to admit that you don't have all the answers. Be more aware of how you think and what you think. What are your real opinions, what have your experiences really taught you?

Since our world is currently swinging towards political fundamentalism, where we all think we have an opinion that is largely informed by the politically biased media we read, it is more important than ever to question what we are being told. Truth is a slippery concept, because adults often lie to themselves and each other. There are layers upon layers of smokescreens shielding us from the truths in our society (and politics), truths that we don't want to see or know—or, if we do know, have no idea how to begin to address them. The more we learn, the more we talk to each other without agenda or defensiveness, the more we will start to see a little of the truth. To me, truth is about authenticity, about seeing the problems in our society, the imperfections and the real, tangible conditions that need to change. You can only start to see them when you let go of your own ego, and try to understand.

Be brave, and think before you leap. Appreciate the people in your lives who read a lot, who think a lot, who have quiet voices but a lot to say. Make room for silence and deep reflection in your life. Don't be afraid of exploring and learning. Talk to people about what you've learnt. Ask them what they think. Make space for people to talk to you about what interests them. You might learn something new.

On Introversion

'The secret to life is to put yourself in the right lighting.
For some it's a Broadway spotlight; for others, a lamplit
desk.'

— Susan Cain, *Quiet.*

L ike any other label, or less-desired personality trait, the word
introvert has a historically negative definition. Words such
as 'shy', 'antisocial', 'anxious', 'reclusive', 'loner', 'secretive',
'overthinker', and 'quiet'—perhaps the most innocuous, but often
most undesired. In the last ten years, there has been a change in
perception, heralded by Susan Cain (the author of *Quiet*) and Laurie
Helgoe (the author of *Introvert Power*, published in 2008), a change
that means introverts can breathe a sigh of relief and finally accept
and understand themselves as they are. More importantly, society at
large is slowly beginning to understand that introverts have gifts of
their own, that being introverted doesn't mean we have no zest for
life, ideas, interesting contributions, or enthusiasm.

Solitude is equated with loneliness in Western society. As a
result, people who enjoy their own company, or need more time
alone to recharge, are viewed with concern—are they sad or
depressed? Do they need cheering up or prodding to lighten up and
socialise? People who are naturally quieter and thoughtful and not

the life and soul of the party are less likely to be included in conversation, thought of as shy or boring. Particularly in communities and societies that don't value the life of the mind, or understand that there are different ways to achieve results. That perhaps that quiet person has the solution for your problems, or the problems of your company. Or that they might have a wild imagination and a dry sense of humour. Often, still waters run deep—you might have a fascinating, mind expanding conversation if you work a little harder.

Introversion is on the opposite side of the scale to extroversion, though it is more common to fall a little more to one side than to be fully introverted or extroverted, or even to be an ambivert. Introverts are not necessarily quiet, shy, and retiring—in fact, we can often be boisterous, lively, and excitable. The key is that we require less stimulation to be satisfied with an activity—whereas extroverts need more stimulation to have the same effect. There are other definitions and traits that are more tenuous and have less of a basis in measurable psychology, and more in social observation and accounts of behaviour, but this seems to be the rule most often accepted.

What does this mean? It means, for example, that if I were to go to a party, I may want to leave earlier because I would want some time alone to recharge and process. This too, is another key trait associated with introverts—we need more time to process and recharge, often alone. This doesn't mean that we always like to be alone. What this means is that perhaps some introverts prefer to socialise in smaller groups, and that they need less time for that socialising, because they don't need as much social stimulation to get the same buzz as extroverts do. It does depend on the situation, however. Introverts can interact for hours with some people; particularly people they are close to, or people that they have shared interests with. Still, at loud, crowded parties, introverts are more likely to want to leave earlier because they become overstimulated and burnt out. It is about picking and choosing the environment in which you flourish the most, which could help you socialise with more confidence.

My own social experiments have helped me to understand what kind of social environments I feel most comfortable in. That doesn't mean I can't deal with other social situations, just that they are more challenging, and often leave me emotionally and mentally exhausted. Parties, whilst they can be fun depending on what kind of party they are—there is a huge difference between small gatherings of friends and large, boisterous gathering of people you don't know—are often the biggest culprit for over-stimulation. There is also my deafness to consider when attending events—will I be able to follow conversations? Will it take more or less effort to lip-read, and will it leave me feeling drained or relaxed? Perhaps being a deaf introvert is a little harder—as well as the draining effort of lip-reading, you are also susceptible to becoming over-stimulated sooner.

On the other hand, introverts often flourish in smaller gatherings, of around two to six people. It is for this reason that I enjoy meeting people one to one, or for cinema trips, meals out, book group meetings, and other activities such as the theatre, cooking for friends and family, or days out. In recent years, I've come to realise that these kinds of meetings suit me the best, and that I am happy to meet new people if it is in smaller groups of mutual friends. I also find that introverts love internet groups—particularly organised into mutual interests—because we can chime in on conversations when it suits us. Since I'm also a blogger, I love to get to know other bloggers through the comment sections of their blogs and mine.

'Where else but cyberspace does the introvert have the opportunity to start in our comfort zone of written communication and talk later? How else can you defy geography and search widely for a soul connection? And because introverts can often open up more easily in a written message, Internet communication can also enhance existing relationships.'

— Laurie Helgoe, *Introvert Power*.

There are also all those supposedly negative traits attached to the word 'introvert'. The first one, 'shy', can be a debilitating thing. Shyness has been identified as a fear of social judgement—that is equally, if not more, likely to be experienced by extroverts too. So we can consider shyness as something that is universal rather than something connected to introversion. Introversion does also not tend towards the traits of being antisocial, reclusive, or a loner. There is nothing wrong with being a loner if that's your thing, but as a rule, most introverts are happy to interact with other people in many different situations.

Social anxiety is also separate to introversion—like shyness, it can be debilitating, but extroverts can also be susceptible. I have experienced both shyness and mild social anxiety, and they don't change the way I become over-stimulated in certain environments, or change my preference for socialising with smaller groups of people. Perhaps it is easier for me to manage social anxiety and shyness with smaller groups (and it is far easier to follow whilst lip-reading), but social anxiety, at its worst, can stop people from wanting to meet anyone at all. I find that if, or when, I become afraid or nervous of meeting friends, I know that I'm experiencing social anxiety.

Many introverts are good listeners, and good at reading body language, although this is something that extroverts can also be good at. Listening well is a skill that you can become better at over time, but often because some introverts find themselves watching and listening, taking in information, rather than talking, they learn a lot about the people they are with. Deaf introverts, in particular, may be extremely good at reading body language and the nuances of behaviour, and if you are a sensitive person, you find yourself gleaning more from an interaction, other than just what is being spoken (or signed). For example, being sensitive to someone else's unspoken mood.

As for the stereotype of the bookish, over-thinking introvert, I can't dispel that for myself (!)—but everyone has a different personality, as well as passions, ideals, and background, and mine just happen to lean heavily on the bookish side. Though I may love to read, I am also a passionate supporter of human and animal rights causes, passionate about arts, culture, and films, and love small, quiet, towns just as much as I love noisy, bustling cities. I often feel like the bookworms amongst us—because of how reading cultivates a passion for life, adventure, and emotion—are often in love with life itself. Introverts, just as extroverts, are a rainbow of difference. You will also find bookish extroverts, and thrill-seeking introverts. Some of the most well-read writers and authors I know are also extroverts. I know of some introverts who love to do daredevil things, such as climbing cliffs and skydiving. So personality and preferences will always differ from person to person, regardless of introversion or extroversion.

As the opening quote to this essay says, not everyone will thrive in, or want to be in the spotlight. Some of us want to pursue rewarding lives and careers away from the glaring light of the stage. Success can be measured in different ways—we define what success means to us individually. Finding our own power comes from becoming wholly ourselves, celebrating our strengths, and not berating ourselves for being something we're not. As Cain writes, spend your free time the way you want to, in a way that feels good to you—don't feel bad for not wanting to go to the party if you don't have the energy, or simply don't want to. Remember that quality is often better than quantity when it comes to friendships—if having many friends, particularly close friends, doesn't work for you, then that is fine.

Though I've found that there is something incredibly freeing and positive that comes from understanding the unique traits of introversion, I'm careful about it, too. I believe that labels are only useful if they help us understand ourselves, and that it's dangerous to label other people unless they feel that they identify with, or feel good about, that label. I feel that it's positive that introversion has been identified as something normal and something to celebrate, yet I also feel that this is not to denigrate extroverts (and ambiverts), who also have their own unique, wonderful traits. Since we live in a society that has traditionally valued so-called extrovert traits for so long, it has been important for introverts to recognise that they're not alone, and that we have just as much right to own our quietness, preferences, and lifestyle. It just so happens that we've coincided with a period in psychology and social science that recognises 'introvert' as a good, positive thing to be.

The Search For Meaning and Purpose

'Vulnerability is the birthplace of love, belonging, joy, courage, empathy, and creativity. It is the source of hope, empathy, accountability, and authenticity. If we want greater clarity in our purpose or deeper and more meaningful spiritual lives, vulnerability is the path.'

— Brené Brown, *Daring Greatly.*

When I was younger, I spent a lot of time pondering philosophical and metaphysical questions, such as 'what is the meaning of life?' and 'what is my purpose?' and 'what does it all mean?'. In adulthood, I am still exploring and asking myself these questions, though my usual answer to the first one is that I believe that the meaning of life is to live—to change, to grow, to learn, to experience, and to express. It is far more complicated than that, once you begin to dig deeper, and look for further philosophies and ideas, for further spiritual meanings. When you choose not to follow any particular religion, and you don't believe that an all-powerful entity has created everything, what does this leave for you?

This is the crux of the matter. The biggest purpose of organised religion, in this secular, individualised time, is to give meaning, routine and spirituality to our lives. It works as an anchor for our lives, when we are going through difficult experiences and need to feel that we have some kind of safety, in a world that often seems dark and unsettling, and yes, unsafe. So, the next question is—what makes us feel safe, what reassures us, when there is something happening that we feel we have no control over? War, death, illness, depression, and politics—how do we make sense of this world?

I used to believe that the pursuit of knowledge, of learning, and education, could give me some of the answers I needed. To an extent, reading books about philosophy, psychology, and sociology, has given me a way of making sense of who I am, who we are, and my place in the world. The key to understanding this world of ours is to read with an enquiring mind, to ask questions, to think about whether something has value for you. There has been an explosion of popular philosophy and psychology books, along with self-help, in recent years, adding further knowledge and tools to our understanding of ourselves and the world around us. Active reading, and learning, means we are constantly adding to our personal growth, and becoming more mature, enlightened human beings.

Still, I'm under no illusions that reading, on its own, necessarily makes you a better person. Where do we learn what is and isn't acceptable, our moral codes, how to know if our world-view needs adjusting? Again, I feel this has a lot to do with having a curious and questioning mind: which constantly seeks to learn about other people, their lives, and to take that leap of empathy. It is always about empathy, in the end—the imaginary stepping into the feelings, thoughts, and lives of other people. This is the only way to understand—to listen. To actively listen to people as they tell their stories. To learn about systems of oppression, privilege, and social justice, we have to be quiet and listen. Morality can be set by parents, religion, and the world you grow up in, but at the same time, this doesn't mean that we can't change and adjust as adults.

Being truly open-minded and in a state of curiosity means that you are more open to seeing what other people might miss. Taking notice of body language, vibes, the unsaid, the unseen—the minute changes around you. Waking up to authenticity, to truth, in life requires effort and to be open requires guarding against being judgemental, and black and white thinking. Life is grey areas, always—even though there is a sliding scale of evil. We know that abuse, murder, war, trafficking, slavery, injustice, lies, and violence are all wrong. I feel that the only way to be open-minded is to understand that you often have to question your own reactions, and accept that sometimes, you can be wrong.

My inclination is always to look underneath, to spot the underlying meanings and patterns. I want to know why something is, where it has come from, and how it happened. Meaning doesn't just come from religion or spiritualism. It can come from anything that gives you an experience, whether this is something physical, emotional, or psychological. Meaning is subjective. Every person has a different world-map, which tells us how to navigate the world. Sometimes we need to adjust it, to write on it, to draw new horizons, even to rip it up and start again. It's all possible. We have to challenge ourselves often to ensure that we are living our lives well, that we are growing and learning, reaching our potential. To live in alignment with our values as much as we can.

Finding purpose is trickier. Some might feel that purpose can come from career and what they do, and to an extent, I feel that way too. Nonetheless, it's too simplistic, and often not fulfilling, to find purpose in work—to believe that is to believe that everyone's purpose is driven by making money. This can't be right. What about if we took away the need for making money? Would you still do the job or work that you are doing? Does it still give you purpose and joy? The answer will be different from person to person, and there is no right answer. The key to purpose must be whatever drives us—perhaps a need to help others, or a belief that what we are doing makes a difference. Or even just something within that pushes us to challenge ourselves, to be better human beings.

Our passions—what we truly love doing—must be considered in this question of purpose. However, not all our passions drive us forward in our lives, or fulfil us. Fulfilment—a sense of contentment—comes when our deepest selves are moving towards some higher state of understanding, whether of ourselves or of the world. Perhaps purpose is more than pursuing our passions, or ambition, or even understanding more deeply. Perhaps it has no real basis in reality, because 'purpose' suggests that we all need to constantly search for something that we might never find. At the same time, we have to make our own meanings, and learn all we can, to feel that we are making the most of our lives.

It is also true that not everything needs to have a purpose. If what motivates us is love, and a need to understand more deeply, then maybe this is the purpose of our lives. To learn how to love: ourselves, the world, and the people in our families, whether by birth or friendship. Love is about bringing out the potential in ourselves and those around us. It is about encouragement, challenge, and understanding. Loving well means we have a groundswell of strength for when we go out into the world, and do whatever it is we want to do. Making mistakes, learning from them–again, maybe our purpose is to learn, try again, and become wiser, more resilient, brave individuals, who can love deeply.

How do we learn to love deeply? We have to recognise the difference between shallow and deep love. Shallow love observes the object of love as a possession, as a mirror of yourself, someone who isn't a separate individual. Whilst love that has the potential to be deeper comes from a place of recognising that you are both individuals, with your own dreams and needs, and that our purpose is to help that person become all it is possible for them to be, to nurture and encourage, to challenge them when needed (gently), and to listen well. Be someone's champion, and let them be yours. It

117

is difficult, and I struggle with these ideals all the time: they also give incredible rewards. Stretch towards love however you can.

Brené Brown, in her books and research on vulnerability, belonging, purpose and imperfection, has written about how vulnerability can be the birthplace of 'love, belonging, joy, courage, empathy, and creativity.' She writes, in *Daring Greatly*, that if we want deeper meaning and clarity of purpose in our lives, we need to be able to be vulnerable. Being vulnerable is about showing our true selves, not hiding away our imperfections, scars, fears, failures, or disappointments. To be all-in with life and connection. Instead of shying away from truth, from the possibility of heartbreak, embracing the struggle and showing up as you are. Not being so afraid that we won't be loved, that we hide our authentic selves away. Particularly, it can be hard in this day and age of social media and political and social divisions to show up in a way that is true to yourself, but with some work and courage—like Brown says, by daring greatly—we can tap into that truth. Being yourself is hard precisely because we are afraid of being seen—in all our imperfection. Purpose and meaning, though, can spring from living your life in a way that is true to you.

My understanding of meaning and purpose are always developing. The main thing for me has been to learn openness, to listen attentively, and to try and stretch my awareness of the world as much as I can. You will have your own ideas about meaning and purpose, but maybe these ideas will help you in some way, to expand your definitions, whatever you believe.

Indolence: The Pleasure of Doing Nothing

In my first year of secondary school (what we in the UK call high school), I had a meeting with my form tutor, my parents, and the head of the HIU (hearing impaired unit), an annual review. All deaf pupils had an annual review—a review of our progress, support needs, and a space for parents, pupils, and teachers to bring up any questions or concerns. At one such review, my form tutor, when giving her opinion about my behaviour at form time (registration and at the end of the day, before the final class), said that she felt that because I didn't put my hand up or answer questions she asked in class, I was lazy. I don't think she meant it as an insult, or as something that couldn't be changed, but the word 'lazy' stuck in my mind. For a deaf pupil, who often worked twice as hard as hearing pupils, lipreading, reading notes from notetakers, and catching up by reading outside class, it felt monumentally hurtful. My support teachers and parents were quick to explain that no, I wasn't lazy—I was anxious about the quiet volume of my voice, and it was hard for me to lipread, particularly if I was tired.

My voice had an awkward habit of either being too quiet, or sticking in my throat because I became so nervous about talking in front of so many people. The hardest thing was that my well-meaning support teachers then took this as a signal to constantly encourage me to answer questions in class, even supplying me with the right answers. For an introvert this would be hard enough, but when you're deaf and also battling shyness, this was humiliating. As a result, I developed a bit of a complex about my voice and how it sounded to others, whilst at the same time, resisting all the efforts of my support teachers to get me to answer questions in class. They encouraged all the other deaf students to answer questions in class too, but I became particularly resentful about it. A mixture of stubbornness and a desire to retain my own autonomy as a teenager meant that it became a sticking point throughout my school career.

Having read Susan Cain's *Quiet: The Power of Introverts in a World That Can't Stop Talking*, I know now that it's a common thing for introverts to hold back and feel resentful if put on the spot, especially when it comes to speaking. It isn't that we don't know what to say, or the answer, but that being put on the spot flusters us, and can result in extra anxiety, and may make our minds go blank. The extra layer of anxiousness about my voice, seeing as it was naturally quiet, meant that it took me many years to get to a point where I felt comfortable voicing my opinions in a group, or feel confident enough to give a university presentation.

The word 'lazy' though, is something I still struggle with. I constantly question myself and wonder if I am lazy. Never mind that all of us struggle with laziness, or let ourselves give in from time to time. Laziness is often paired with other words, since us humans like to stereotype. My size, my tiredness from lip-reading and paying attention, and my quietness may have given people, over the years, the impression that I'm lazy. Why is laziness seen as such a negative thing? We associate it with idleness, with laxness, not having direction or purpose. In the twenty-first century, with the advent of Netflix and binging on TV series, there is a tongue-in-cheek acceptance of the art of laziness—which even Netflix itself likes to guilt us about ('Are you still watching The Big Bang Theory?' Absolutely!).

At heart, perhaps all we want is to be laid-back, swinging apes, lazing in the sunshine, eating bananas and grooming. Nevertheless, as humans, we also possess restlessness, a need to move, for progress. It isn't enough for us to just exist and revel in the fact of our existence. We need to do something with it, in a way that fulfils and contents us. For it to be assumed that we are lazy may have a kernel of truth, because we do possess the desire for it, but we are also constantly striving, seeking knowledge, self-improvement, connection, and growth. The energy within us moves towards life and activity, rather than just being.

As a young teenager, being called lazy was perhaps a bigger insult than it was meant to be, in part because of the sheer amount of effort I had to make—that deaf people in general have to make—to keep up with their hearing peers in and outside class. It was also an insult against difference, against the different abilities people have to give the world. Not everyone is going to be an accomplished speaker. It can be worked upon, and improved, but if someone's strengths lie elsewhere, perhaps teachers can learn to nurture those aspects of a child's skills. At that point in my history, though, I didn't have these insights, which is why teachers need to understand the different ways that their students learn.

When you are a writer, or within the creative industry, it can be very tempting to give in to what we could call 'resistance' but is in fact our lazy monkey mind wanting nothing more than to eat bananas and swing in the trees. It bounces from one thought to another, refuses to settle, drives us towards frustration, and distracts us in a cycle of procrastination. This is why, many a day, I find myself not beginning work when I've planned to begin—on some days, it takes me until 3pm to finally open up Word and begin writing. It's a real thing, this lazy resistance. It pushes at us every day, demanding we give up, down tools, and take a siesta.

Half the battle of doing anything is the strength to silence this aspect of our brains, and learning how to distract it, and quiet it down. The only real way I know how, so far, is to commit to sitting at my desk, and doing something. Often you just have to start with something practical—for me this is the act of painting, drawing, writing in my diary or journal, or doing some photography. Access the part of yourself that wants to create. At my most frustrated, I've also baked cakes and tried new recipes, just to distract my mind into doing something—anything—rather than a frozen, frustrated idleness.

Perhaps some of us are more prone to indolence than others. I know that, given a choice (especially on a rainy day), I would rather curl up with a book and a cup of tea than go for a long walk in the woods. This isn't to say that I don't enjoy walking in the woods. It could be that some of us are more driven by mood and follow our emotions—we know that going for that walk would be good for us, and even inspiring, yet we are also drawn towards the easiness of staying put and reading. I'm no stranger to pyjama days, in fact, I think pyjama days are sometimes necessary because they allow us to recharge and store up our brain energy (they are also necessary for the pure joy and cosiness of it). When you are self-aware and understand when it is time for you to take action, you will. If it matters to you, you will, and can, do it. Maybe this is what being an adult means—knowing when it is time to get dressed and show up. To take responsibility when you need to.

At the heart of it all is the idea of will. How can you have a strong will and yet also be prone to indolence? I can't answer that question. Humans, like Walt Whitman wrote, contradict themselves, and contain multitudes. We can hold opposing forces within us, opposing ideas, opposing traits. How much time we give to them is a matter for how willing you are to give in, and whether you can accept those opposing traits. I accept that I can be indolent, but also that I am a hard worker. I accept that I love curling up to read, but I also accept that I love being in nature, and walking through a canopy of trees. Sometimes I give in and have a day off for reading and watching films—whilst other days I work all day. Balance, as always, is key.

In the film and book *Eat, Pray, Love*, Elizabeth Gilbert is informed by the Italian people she is with that Americans (and perhaps British) people don't know how to take time to savour life, to take something just because—to relax and just be, and appreciate what life has to offer. Although the stereotype of 'dolce far niente' (the art of doing nothing) doesn't reflect the reality of life for most Italians— of course Italian people have a mix of hard-working and less productive people in their society (like all places do)—it still remains an interesting concept. The people Gilbert encountered explained that Americans feel they have to 'earn' the pleasures they get in life, like a cold beer, or good food. 'Dolce far niente', on the other hand, demands it all, just because it is there in life—the art of relaxing into sheer pleasure, the joy of idleness. Part of this is to understand the difference between indolence and appreciating the little joys in life—the pleasure of taking an afternoon to read a book, a stroll in the park, a delicious coffee or cup of tea and a slice of cake, and an evening spent laughing with a friend and drinking a glass of wine. You don't have to 'earn' them. They are often the reason for life, at times. To learn to relax, you have to learn to be lazy and sink into pleasurable moments.

If I'm having a week where I'm constantly frustrated and stressed, I have to check in with myself and understand why. I live in a culture of extremes—one which, as I mentioned, binges on Netflix and box-sets, spends hours on the internet, and seeks entertainment, and one in which 'I'm busy' is seen as a badge of honour, an essential, even desirable thing. Frantic, progress driven busy-ness is not necessarily a sign of a life well lived. Seeking constant entertainment ignores the value of stillness, and just being—moments of quiet and reflection. Perhaps the crux of my argument here is that slowing down is good, essential—and that at times, we have to give ourselves permission to be lazy—and to protect that laziness as time we give ourselves to enjoy the art of pleasure.

On Fear

All writers and creators come up against fear. It's there, in the background, waiting to trip you up. I've had many battles with fear: from the imaginative fear you have as a child, to the soul-crushing paralysis that can set in as an adult. Fear is different to depression, or anxiety. Anxiety is a ramped-up form of fear, which is often treatable and can be managed, whilst fear often has a purpose, and can be less debilitating.

It's a part of human nature, being afraid—telling us when we are in danger. It keeps us safe and cautious when we need to be. But the boundary is when fear is no longer about keeping us safe, but keeping us from doing something new, something that may seem scary, but has positive, life enriching outcomes. For example, writing a novel. We worry about what other people think. We feel that our writing isn't good. We are afraid of being laughed at or judged.

It's a matter of faith, to step out into a place we don't know in the dark, where we don't know what the outcome will be. It's about getting comfortable with the unknown, with the feeling of no control. In the case of a novel, it is about forgetting about people's unknown reactions. Fear lies to us—tells us that you're right to be afraid, because nobody could possibly want to read this. It searches for the negative explanation, and seizes on those thoughts as confirmation for why you are feeling like this. When it is, really, about the way the chemicals in our body react to difficult tasks, and the relationship we have with fear, our own particular inner critic.

If you're an adrenaline junkie, you'll probably know how exciting it is to be afraid, to be on the precipice of whatever exhilarating activity you're doing. You harness that fear as a good thing, as something that drives you and makes you feel invigorated. Whilst the more mundane kind of fear, the fear that frequently stops us from taking action, is unpleasant, and makes you feel like you've failed. I do daily battle with that kind of fear. There are a few different kinds of fear I've noticed I brush up against and live with.

The first one is the doubting type of fear—for example, the fear that I'll never write anything good. The aim of this is to stop me from writing. All I have to do to push through this is remind myself of what I have written, which has received positive feedback. This can also manifest itself in self-doubt—doubting that I'm right about something, doubting that I have what it takes to stay on a course of action, my self-worth, and so on. It can be turned around if you can find reasons why it's not true, and prove to yourself that, in fact, you are more than capable of doing whatever it is that this fear is stopping you from doing.

Another one is social fear. This is more complicated, and for me, brushes up against social anxiety. For a deaf person, especially, this can be incredibly difficult to manage, because as well as feeling nervous and afraid of certain kinds of social situations (large groups, crowds, noisy environments, new people, shyness), you have to deal with communication—whether that is lip-reading, BSL (British Sign Language), or needing a quiet environment. Being someone prone to deep shyness and social anxiety, coupled with a preference for small groups, this can make social situations a major issue. However—I have, over the years, come to find different ways of coping. As a rule, I do try to avoid situations where I know I will end up feeling terrible afterwards—large groups of people I don't know (small groups or one-to-one is much better)—and being in crowded, noisy and chaotic spaces. I do like meeting new people occasionally, and I know that, despite my nervousness, the only way I'm going to meet like-minded people is by taking that initiative.

There are some situations you can't control, and for those, you just have to find the best possible ways of managing them. You don't have to talk to everyone. You don't have to be anything other than yourself. I have to give myself a pep-talk in situations I don't have much control over, and remind myself that nobody is going to judge me, and if they do, well, that's their loss. I don't believe that you can size someone up on the first meeting.

It has always been my belief that to get to know people, it takes longer than one or two meetings and, especially with introverts and shy or socially anxious people, it can take longer. The same can be said of deaf and hard of hearing people—there is an adjustment period to allow for communication. It takes me a few times to get used to lip-reading someone, and unfortunately, sometimes that never happens, which adds another aspect of worry to a social encounter. I've learnt that I just have to go with the flow, and what happens, happens—there is no perfect social situation, because we're all imperfect humans trying our best.

The third type of fear is resistance (and procrastination). It's similar to doubting fear, in that it stops you from doing what you want or need to do, but is something that might become less over time depending on how you deal with it. If left unchecked, it can turn into paralysis, which I've experienced and would do anything to avoid happening again. Taking writing as an example, resistance makes you drag your heels, makes the task at hand seem extremely hard work, and tells you that there are easier, more short term pleasures or tasks you could be doing that are immediately gratifying.

It might be that on any given day, I have a list of tasks I want to do. The top one might be writing, and I may also have reading, research, and photography on the list. Rather than writing, I'll busy myself with the other tasks, or lose time doing something that might seem good to start with, but when the time is gone, will make me feel as if I've wasted it. This is a classic case of what Natalie Goldberg, the author of *Writing Down The Bones*, calls 'monkey mind'—the easily distracted, short term pleasure mind that ignores the rewards of long-term, focused tasks.

What works for me is two strategies. Firstly, journaling, freewriting, or an 'information dump'—allowing that 'monkey mind' free rein to just write itself out. It focuses my mind on something other than the task at hand, but doesn't mean I'm focusing on something other than writing. With something else, that might mean giving yourself a way in to the task at hand. Basically, just doing something that needs focus—perhaps doodling, or a creative activity that doesn't involve using a screen or your phone, a 'way in' to your work. With this, I try to turn off my phone and use an internet-limiting application like Freedom, so that I minimise the distractions.

Secondly, focusing on a physical activity, such as baking, making something with your hands, going for a walk, doing some form of gentle exercise, or doing something that is the opposite of what you are doing (eg. instead of writing, painting or photography). This refreshes your mind, changes the tempo of your day, and may even give you some ideas (and allows you to think). It helps me to unblock any resistance because I'm moving, doing an activity, but not one that means I'm being distracted by the internet or doing something that will use up all my time. It busies and hopefully tires out the 'monkey mind', and gives you the freedom to think clearly and focus.

There is a difference between the kind of anxiety that stops you living your life, and the lower level, but still uncomfortable anxiety that can be managed with just a few tools, like the ones I've mentioned above. Debilitating anxiety may need professionals to help you through—whether with support and medication, or through mindfulness and other forms of therapy. I feel that our society is slowly becoming more aware of the stigma surrounding mental health, anxiety, and depression, though we still have a long way to go. Matt Haig's recent book, *Notes on a Nervous Planet*, for example, shows us that the conversation around anxiety and the conditions of modern society that can amplify it, is entering the public arena, no longer something shameful to hide away. In some cultures, and countries, there is still so much stigma and misinformation, and I hope that if you feel alone or are suffering from anxiety, you know that you are not alone, and that there is nothing to be ashamed of.

Fear is a remnant of our evolutionary past. Whilst it has its uses (caution, instinct, warning of real danger), in our modern world, it can be difficult to deal with everything that life throws at us, and it can become difficult to cope: yet fear is something that can be understood, accepted, and managed.

For The Dreamers

D reamers imagine what life could be, the possibilities in every cloud and every person. They look beyond: beyond what is. They try their hardest to birth dreams into being. There is nothing idealistic about being a dreamer. Idealism is different—idealism is wanting your ideals to shape the world, to mould the world into a certain paradigm.

What does it mean, to have a dream? Martin Luther King had a dream. He dreamt that the world could be a better, peaceful, more loving place, for people of colour and the rest of the world. He dreamt that there would be no more war, no more violence. He dreamt of more joy and friendship. Of change that could achieve true equality and liberation from the conditions of society that divide and oppress. And what did John Lennon and Yoko Ono believe? That it was possible to imagine a world, too, that had no war and hate, full of love.

We need those dreamers. The ones that, in times of fear and anxiety, show us that hope remains. That even in the darkness of death and violence, life can still be beautiful, and full of joy. That choosing optimism, choosing to focus on gratitude, yet seeing what can be better, and imagining how it could be, is the way forward. Cynicism is the bitterness of giving up, believing that we have no power. We have power: we just need to know in what ways— because we all have a different kind of power within us. We can choose how to use that power, to use it in ways that lift us all up.

Activists need to dream. If we can't imagine what we are fighting for—what a liberated world could look like—we will lose hope. To dream of something different, something that is better than now, and work towards that, is essential. All the ground gained in the fight for human rights, liberation and equality began with seeing what could be different, what could be better. In many ways, dreaming can keep us alive. A dream becomes a goal, which is broken down to achievable actions. In dreamland, nothing is impossible. We live in dreamland—just look around with new eyes, noticing every invention, every idea, every piece of art that surrounds us.

Dreamers may sometimes have their head in the clouds. In the drift back to the ground, they carry ideas, new understandings, and another way to express something. Some dreamers are also practical, pragmatic. They know how to bring something into being, and who can help them. They share thoughts, ideas, and creations. We have to believe that even just helping one person, even just inspiring one human being, is worth the struggle. Working together towards a common dream, a possible reality, strengthens bonds of connection.

It takes bravery and determination to be a dreamer. To give yourself to the world, to show your inner life to others. Bravery is not just large acts, it is the small, brave actions we take every day in our lives. Fear is along for the ride, and tells us not to show so much of ourselves, and the bravery is always to acknowledge that, and share anyway. Grow towards vulnerability, towards being your true self. Let go of the fear, the imposter syndrome, the self-doubt—you deserve to be all that you can be.

Don't be swayed by those who tell you that this harsh, unforgiving, violent world is no place for dreaming. Everything you have, everything around us, was once someone's dream. We live, every day, in other people's dreams become manifest. Possibility is everywhere—every moment is a chance to take a leap into the unknown and bring your dreams to life. Other dreamers will help. Other dreamers will spur you on. Look to the people who inspire you, and let their words, their art, their creations, show you that yes—you can do that too.

If one dream doesn't work, there are others. There are so many. Our capacity for dreaming and love are infinite. We change, little by little, every day. When we look up into the sky, the big blue, or the glittering blanket of stars, we can see that infinity, and bring that sense of wonder back into our lives, that sense of millions of years of dreams and ideas. Give yourself a chance to wonder. Give yourself a chance to take flight. Remember, always, that you are not alone—that a universe of dreamers are with you.

Surfacing

Learning to swim again after so long underwater is a painstaking process. To swim again, you need to remember what it means to breathe. Taking one breath after another, drawing in the exposed, sharp air, is pain. Swimming again is remembering how to feel. This is why each breath feels like a stab in the lungs.

Grief has a way of becoming too much, so much that you can't bear it. Instead of moving through the grief, instead of sitting with it and looking it in the eyes, you avert your gaze and turn off the tap. You stop feeling. You think, somewhere deep down, that you are protecting yourself. Maybe. Maybe it's a way of standing still for a while. Sometimes in life, to live is to learn about suffering, and how to go within it and come out the other side with a new understanding.

It hurts, this learning. You have to give yourself space for it. You can't brush it off and pretend that everything is fine. Believe me, I have experienced some stretches of time in my life internalising my pain and pretending to others that everything is good, that I am okay. I have, at times, isolated myself, hiding the ugly, painful, dark, storing it away for moments I am alone. You can't live like that. There is always someone who will listen, who will help you to bear the darkness better, will start you towards the light of healing.

Admitting that you need help is strong, and trying to cope alone, trying to surface from the depths without someone else encouraging you, is much harder.

At the same time, swimming to shore is ultimately your own journey to take. You can have all the support you need, but to live again, to map out a course that makes sense to you, and to take those first painful, deep breaths, is yours alone. Allowing yourself to feel again is a revolution. A small revolution, but one that feels like an explosion of colour in your otherwise dull, grey, world. I know those revolutions. I have had many of them. I always swim towards feeling as opposed to the depths of apathy. Feeling can be exhausting, which is why humans can be prone to sinking.

You will need ventilation systems for breathing. The type of systems that fill you up and remind you that life is worth living. For me, it has always been reading and writing. I have had moments of pure will when I read one book after another, determined to make myself feel, to keep searching for myself within the pages of other people's stories. It is true that fiction is a way to travel towards ourselves. It is a succession of choices, of emotions. The peril and soul-searching the characters go through mirror the internal changes taking place within you. They are stories of people finding themselves, of going through metamorphoses. If you feel their pain, think their thoughts, empathise—there is hope. Hope that emotion, no matter the severity, can break through the grey.

One spring, after my seventh book, I had felt almost every emotion I was possible of feeling. I no longer felt that there was too much pain—I welcomed every small fleeting feeling. Even though some of the books I had read—like *The Goldfinch* by Donna Tartt—seemed unbearably painful. It came with recognition that I would rather feel too much than feel nothing. I forced myself to see that in order to find my way back to myself, I would need to accept that pain and emotion might be a heavy burden to bear but that they were a reason for living, and as changeable as the weather. Understanding this helped me to kick harder, to finally break the surface and allow hope back in.

The cold grey numbness is what I have come to recognise as apathy, as a world devoid of meaning and passion. That is what I fight within myself some days. Thankfully less now that I know what I need. This is what makes it hard for people to understand—depression is not necessarily sadness, nor is it just being 'low'—I see it as a colourless, apathetic state of being. Nobody experiences depression in the same way. After the deluge of emotion, of pain, the tsunami, comes the nothingness, stuck in the depths. My strategy is to burrow deep into literature, to write it all out, no matter how tiring it is to go around in circles. You do what you need to do, to travel back to yourself. To reach the shore again.

When grey skies descend again, I seek solace in my journal, in the people who know me best, and the escape and life raft of books—poetry, novels, non-fiction by people who have been through the tumultuous ocean themselves. Over time, you begin to see what patterns lead to sinking. You can recognise when you're overloaded with too much—a racing mind, a sad, broken heart—and reel yourself in. For some, this will mean knowing when to seek help. For others, it will mean using everything in your toolbox to take care of yourself. After all, depression lies to us—it tells us that we are worthless, to be ashamed, that nobody wants to know, or cares. In the worst moments, it tells us that life is pointless, that everything is too hard and it would be easier to let go.

These are the biggest lies, the most destructive ones, which we have to guard ourselves against. Be kind to yourself, boost the positive, calm, and compassionate voices within. Seek compassionate people who will listen. They exist and you can access them. Hug an animal, hug a friend, hug yourself. Seek a sense of comfort—wrap yourself in huge blankets or duvets, watch something that doesn't require much energy to watch, and read the books that you've read many times and know inside out. Write it all out—everything—nobody is going to see that writing, it's just for you. You're fighting for your life, and it's always worth it.

The Real Meaning of Inclusion

Inclusion, at its best, is meant to signify equality, feeling included, being part of something that matters to you, or that matters in whatever situation you are in. The opposite of inclusion, exclusion, can lead to feeling isolated, discarded, unwanted, or forgotten.

In terms of civil rights, inclusion is meant to be about ensuring that everyone can take part to the best of their ability, that they are not left out, unable to participate. In the broadest terms, a government with its citizens' best interests at heart will do everything they can to ensure equal opportunity and access. They should do everything they can to empower people in education, the workplace, health, and housing. In the UK, this is why the NHS and the welfare state were set up—to ensure that all citizens could have access to quality healthcare and, when facing hard times and other issues (such as a change in health, disability, and so on), would be able to manage better.

I've been part of a number of different incarnations of inclusion. In the sense that I'm a citizen of the UK, I'm entitled to and have been entitled to various rights enshrined by law, including healthcare delivered by the NHS, state education, certain state benefits, and civil rights protected by the Human Rights Act, which preserves entitlement to equal treatment, respect, fairness, and dignity. Unfortunately, governments with an agenda are always seeking to erode those rights and replace them or scrap them altogether to further their own mandate, whether or not this harms citizens (particularly those who aren't in the top earning 10% of the world).

With education, the picture for deaf people becomes more complicated (and here I use deaf to include HOH, BSL deaf, and partially deaf). There are different types of education available—mainstream schools which have some kind of support system, often from PDS (Provision for Deaf Students) units (which used to be called HIUs, Hearing Impaired Units), or schools for deaf students, such as Mary Hare or Blanche Nevile. Individual students in mainstream schools without a PDS may be eligible for support through their council, but parents still have to fight for their child's right to get that support without going to either of the two 'usual' options. I went to a mainstream school with an HIU (back in the late 90s, early 00s), and as a result, a certain kind of inclusion was in effect. Much of the time, social life can be a major challenge for deaf children in mainstream schools, unless they are naturally confident and feel supported by their peers. Conversely, they are supported well academically, and will hopefully develop to the best of their abilities.

My gut instinct is to feel that mainstreaming as inclusion doesn't work as well as it could. I had all kinds of issues, from friendship problems, bullying, and developing (undiagnosed) anxiety. I felt like a person split down the middle—my persona at school was at odds with the one I had at home and in the world beyond school. Too much prompting by well-meaning support teachers gave me a complex about my voice, and I felt overly exposed and recognised by peers because I had the label 'deaf': not necessarily what you want when going through the difficult teenage years.

What would real inclusion have looked like in a school setting? Perhaps more freedom to choose—to choose whether or not to sit at the front of the class, or whether or not to put my hand up to answer a question. To feel less like a curiosity in a sea of hearing teenagers.

Still, I am grateful for the education I received—I had a number of inspiring teachers and had the chance to study Sociology, Art, and English Literature. The most important thing, in the end, is having access to education, and having teachers that inspire a passion for learning.

One of the best incarnations of inclusion I have been part of is Chickenshed Theatre. My sister and I grew up performing on stage in plays, musicals, and cabarets. Their ethos has always been about inclusion, in the best sense of the word—they regularly bring out the best potential in the children and adults they work with. This includes everyone from diverse backgrounds, various abilities, and of all genders. They work with ensemble casts, so they actually do try to make sure everyone is included in a performance, particularly for their annual Christmas shows, and some of their spring shows and cabarets. The overarching feeling is that whilst there, you become part of a family, and it's difficult to leave their ethos behind when you go out into the world.

Their idea of inclusion comes extremely close to the universal ideal of inclusion. This is everyone working together to make the world a better, more hopeful, and more thoughtful place, where everyone achieves their potential and doesn't step on anyone else in the process. It is also about adapting the environment and using access tools to include people who need them (such as speech to text or BSL interpreters), eliminating access barriers. It seems like a pipe-dream when the world around us is as volatile and violent as it is. That isn't the only story, though. I know enough people who challenge the perception that the world is falling apart: the perception that nobody is going to make anything better, that nothing is going to change. The people I know wouldn't dream of excluding or judging anyone. There are people and organisations doing superlative things to bring people together and change the way we see the world and behave.

Within the disability rights movement, inclusion is a cultural and intellectual concept (as well as encompassing the removal of environmental barriers). The aim is for disabled people to become more visible, to normalise diversity, across all levels of society. Rather than as 'inspiration' or as objects of 'pity', disabled people are aiming to be seen as the human beings they are, with all the quirks and complexity that comes with humanity. The 'othering' of people, such as people with disabilities, on the whole, comes from a lack of everyday exposure to a variety of cultures, different physical attributes, and complex or positive media portrayals. If we think about the language we use around disability in this country—taking 'benefit scroungers', as one example—you can see how the media stokes the fires of ignorance. Some media has made great strides forwards, but for every positive gain, there is a negative leap backwards.

This is why activists continue to be vocal and campaign tirelessly. Inclusion in this context is not about 'overcoming' and 'achieving', but rather being seen as a part of a diverse, multicultural society: acceptance. This is at odds with most societies across the world, and inclusion is increasingly derided on both the right and left of conventional thought—the right usually favours medical fixes and cures (as well as dismantling policies that protect human rights), whilst inclusion can be seen as another aspect of 'identity' politics by an increasingly neoliberal left.

Far from just being a 'buzzword', I feel that inclusion is a progressive concept, or at least a concept that needs to be reclaimed: one that seeks to further the wellbeing and autonomy of all human beings. The work of inclusion is hard, but not impossible. Some societies and environments are more inclusive than others, utilising universal design (including accessible adaptations in the building of environments), being aware of various access needs, being aware of different cultural and social barriers, whilst others are still in the early stages of understanding the concept. Even in cities like London, inclusion is still not quite the norm—particularly in terms of access for deaf and disabled people. Take the Underground as an example—tannoy announcements without text, a lack of lifts for wheelchairs, a generally chaotic environment that could be overwhelming for people on the autistic spectrum. Awareness is growing, and the internet and more access to different types of media mean that there is more opportunity for education. Still, the way society and government operate in the UK means that there are still major issues with welfare, meaning that deaf and disabled people, people on a lower income, elderly, and younger generations are missing out on basic human rights—safe housing, independence, food, and healthcare. If the government continues to erode the welfare state, this will roll back inclusion for decades, rippling through generations to come.

This is why those of us who can need to fight hard for these essential human rights. In whatever way we can, we have to fight for a better world, no matter whether or not we will see progress in our lifetime. In the end, hope and small gains are important. Big changes come from small changes, building up and rolling down the hill until they collide and hit their target. If we give up just because it seems hopeless, nobody will gain any ground, and we will continue to lose the progress and rights that generations of people have fought for. Short term thinking, particularly in terms of society and human rights, creates disasters and humanitarian crises.

This is why we must do our best to understand the outcome of the changes taking place around us, and what we can do. The work of inclusion needs everyone to change their hearts and minds, to understand each other better, to work harder at seeing each other as human.

Highly Sensitive People

'You're too sensitive, you need to toughen up,' and 'I've got a thick skin, I don't let anything bother me,' are familiar statements, said often enough, that until my mid-twenties, I thought there was something wrong with me. I believed I cared a little 'too much': I could gauge the emotional vibes of other people, would take things to heart, and noticed subtleties in the environment and with other people. Loud, busy places drained me of energy and left me overstimulated, or, at the worst, having a mild panic attack. Minor arguments would leave me weighed down with guilt and sadness. Events and situations that didn't seem to bother other people affected me adversely.

For some time, I believed that being sensitive was a hindrance rather than a characteristic that allowed me to be aware of nuances, grey areas, and subtle emotions. I felt that I didn't have the tools that other people had in order to navigate this busy, loud, and often harsh world. Had I missed a trick along the way? Was it because I was deaf and had missed certain opportunities: to learn about how to cope with situations that hearing people could manage? Or because the 'loss' of one sense heightened the others? Was it because I was undeveloped in some way?

The answer became clearer a few years ago, once again, after reading Susan Cain's *Quiet: The Power of Introverts in a World That*

Can't Stop Talking—a landmark book for many reasons. I became more aware of how certain situations drained my energy and that I needed time to recharge and process my experiences. Yet introversion didn't fully explain my emotional landscape, my awareness of other people's emotions, body language, and how I would often empathise to the point of taking on other people's emotions, blurring too many boundaries and becoming overwhelmed. How I often felt that I lacked a certain armour that other people had.

My sister is also similar in this respect. We're both sensitive, become overwhelmed with too much stress, and are prone to burning out when we take on too much. Through our conversations and separate reading, we came across a psychological concept, HSP, the Highly Sensitive Person. Far from being a new-agey, popular psychology concept, HSPs are people with nervous systems that are more easily overwhelmed. The scientific name is Sensory Processing Sensitivity, SPS. You don't have to be an introvert to be a HSP; there are many extroverts who are HSPs too. Elaine N. Aron's book and psychological studies have delved deeper into the science and behaviour of being HSP, and her book, *The Highly Sensitive Person*, was a revelation to both my sister and me. It explained much that I didn't understand about myself and my reactions, the way I felt about certain situations, and why I became overwhelmed so easily when other people managed without any stress whatsoever.

An HSP, according to Aron, is someone who: could be prone to being overwhelmed by bright lights, strong smells, coarse fabrics, sirens and loud noises, possibly becomes rattled when having a lot to do in a short amount of time, may make a point of avoiding violent films and TV shows, withdraws somewhere (a darkened room, for example) to get relief when overwhelmed with a situation, makes it a priority to arrange life around avoiding upsetting or overwhelming situations, notices and enjoys delicate or fine scents, tastes, sounds, or works of art, possesses a rich and complex inner life, and may have been labelled as shy or sensitive by teachers or parents when young.

These characteristics work as examples to illustrate the general facets of being HSP. It has been recognised, by scientists, as a biological and innate survival strategy found in over 100 species, that amounts to being more observant before acting. It isn't a new discovery, but has been misunderstood by being labelled as inhibitedness, fearfulness, or neuroticism, according to Aron's research. She writes that some HSPs can behave in these ways, but it isn't actually innate to behave like this if you have the trait; and in cultures where sensitivity isn't valued, HSPs often have low self-esteem because they are told to 'not be so sensitive'.

The facets of Sensory Processing Sensitivity are scientifically abbreviated to DOES—Depth of Processing, Overstimulation, Emotional responsivity and empathy, and Sensitive to Subtleties.

Depth of processing describes the way that people with SPS take longer to cognitively process situations and answers, and have a tendency towards observation before joining in. This often makes them appear shy and withdrawn, perhaps even cold and detached. In fact, within the brain of someone with SPS, you might find that they are 'taking things in', considering how they can contribute, thinking deeply about their answers, or needing some time to acclimatise to the energy of the situation. Sometimes, people with SPS may just want to soak in the atmosphere without being too involved in the festivities, as opposed to diving right in and being the life and soul of the party (at least right away – remember that some HSPs are extroverts!). This doesn't mean that they don't have anything to offer, just that they take longer, and think deeper, or that they don't contribute unless they are sure they have a beneficial answer or action.

Overstimulation, as discussed briefly before, is connected to gaining so much stimulation—sensory related (noise, light, movement, crowds, etc), or emotion related (excitement, happiness, sadness, grief, and so on)—that people with SPS need some time to regroup, decompress, and be alone to rest. Far from being a luxury, this time works to help the brain make sense of an overwhelming situation. Conversely, what is overwhelming to someone with SPS might not be overwhelming to someone without. This is probably a frustrating aspect of the trait for people in the lives of someone with SPS—their tendency to become frustrated, tearful, burnt-out, anxious or irritated by a situation or experience that has overwhelmed them. This is not to say that someone with SPS is always tearful and emotional—we develop coping strategies and learn to know our limits—but that it's something to be aware of.

For example, a parent of a child with SPS might need to learn how to reassure and not push a child into something that they are overly fearful of. Instead, introduce them to new experiences in stages, in ways that isn't forceful. This helps to create space for their comfort zone to expand, and will allow them to develop at their own pace. Children with SPS might also have more inexplicable tantrums, being labelled as a 'bad' child, when they are just extremely overwhelmed. In that case, a parent may need to allow the child to decompress somewhere quiet, then discuss why that behaviour was difficult and their reasons for it later on, after they are less overwhelmed. For adults with SPS, it might mean learning how to dip their toes into new experiences in stages too—to learn, process, then slowly get used to doing something different, being somewhere different, or meeting new people.

Emotional responsivity and empathy illustrates the way that many people with SPS often have deep emotional responses, and are more prone to feeling deep empathy for other people, animals, and situations in the world. They are likely to consider, for example, how they can best use their skills to work with people (or/and animals) to make the world a better place. They might consider kindness and compassion to be a part of their moral code. It could be that they are moved deeply by works of art, literature, music, theatre, films, and other creative performance. They may also find it incredibly difficult to deal with situations that involve constant conflict and stress.

Being sensitive to subtleties, someone with SPS may notice details that other people miss. These details may come from the environment, the body language of other people, noticing emotional vibes, changes in light, temperature, or mood, subtle tastes and smells, touch and sounds, perhaps a strongly developed peripheral vision. Or they may be extremely detail oriented in the work they do, considering every scenario, being prone to perfectionism, or investigating different possibilities. In some ways, being this sensitive to detail offsets the difficult aspects of SPS – being prone to overstimulation, for example.

Learning that you might have SPS means that you learn tools to work with the traits you have, and how to learn to adapt yourself and your lifestyle to suit, so you become less overwhelmed. It means that you might learn how to use boundaries, and recognise when you need some time out, and not feel bad about your needs. It also means recognising your own particular skills and gifts, and learning how to use them effectively. People with SPS make up 20% of the world's population—our skills and traits are needed for balance. SPS is a collection of traits, not an indication that we are somehow better than people without SPS—we are just different, and have different skills to offer. The problem comes when, because the traits of sensitivity can be devalued by society and educators, HSPs lose their confidence, self-esteem, and feel a lack of purpose.

It can be easy for people who are HSPs to lose their confidence and sense of direction when they are confronted with a society that devalues their contributions. Not everybody is going to be happy doing the same in life, particularly if what they are doing doesn't suit their nature and temperament. In a career and work sense, HSPs will most likely hate open plan offices with a passion, for example, and will thrive in environments where they are able to retreat and process information in their own time. It is possible for HSPs to work in fast paced careers—a sort of fake-it-til-you-make-it situation, but they are more prone to overwhelm, so this is something that needs to be considered when choosing careers and creating a life that works for them. This is a good case for learning your own limits and what adaptations you can make to build resilience and understand your own needs.

This is why it's so important, just as it is to value introversion, that HSPs are given the chance to flourish and understand their own trait. Better self-awareness and understanding will allow someone with SPS to see how they can use their trait in a positive, life-affirming way, to manage the difficult aspects, and thrive.

Part Four:

Writing and Creating

Why Write?

Nearing completion of this book, I am now using my twelfth notebook since I started writing again in 2011. Writing in these notebooks—which is now a dusty stack of hardbacks, with bent spines, looking thicker than they did when they hadn't been used—marked my transition from beginner writer to seasoned, yet still learning, writer. These notebooks can be counted as one of the few indulgences I allow myself on a limited budget (along with books, tea, and the occasional clothing purchase). For a while, I chose to buy Moleskine notebooks, seduced by their smooth, acid-free pages, weight, and iconic name. My current notebook, however, is an emerald green Leuchtturm 1917, with plain, unlined pages. It marks a different direction, away from the constraints of lined pages, with marginally more space to write, and the possibility of drawing, illustrating, and sticking other materials in. Still an indulgence, but at least I have more space. There is a sense of wonder, looking at this stack of notebooks—at how much my writing has changed and developed over time, as I have grown and changed as a person. They are a record of my disappointments, achievements, and thought-process, scraps of poetry, a place to psychoanalyse myself and let out any difficult emotions, and a place to write down unfledged ideas.

I began writing again because I had an epiphany whilst writing the thesis for my Master's degree. I was working on a social study about deaf women, autobiography, and the intersection of identity (being women, and being deaf). Reading the respondents' autobiographical writings, and reading published autobiographies by deaf women, stirred something that had been dormant for some time. Once I started writing about my experiences as a deaf woman, it opened up a dialogue between myself and the blank page. You could say that Women's Studies—and feminism—brought me back to writing. In truth, it was a collection of moments that led me to think more clearly about what I wanted, and what I wanted for the future. What did I think I had to offer the world? What would my contribution be?

It took a couple more years to truly find my feet with writing. To start with, it was new and exciting, and I bought a library of books about the writing craft, the writing life, freelance writing, and books of essays by writers. I subscribed to Mslexia, the magazine for women who write (I still do – it's a brilliant resource), and to blogs by writers and about writing. I sought out indie writers and followed my favourite authors on Twitter. In short, I immersed myself wholeheartedly into the writing world. I took part in and completed two NaNoWriMo challenges (National Novel Writing Month), a whole month of writing a terrible draft of a novel (or non-fiction book)—and racked up 100,000 words of unfinished writing altogether. I felt that I would go back to those novels and develop and finish them, but they are sitting in my drafts folder, still unfinished five years later. Maybe I will look at and mine them for inspiration and ideas sometime, but they represent a time when I didn't fully accept that I needed time to develop my voice and style before I jumped fully into writing a novel in a month. They were experiments, and still worth those two Novembers I spent writing them.

Blogging was a constant throughout these six years of learning. If I look back at my earliest blog posts, and a recent blog post, the style has become more nuanced, deeper, and mature. Experience—life experience, and learning—have brought me to a place where I am a little more confident in my own voice, and trusting that what I write may not be perfect, but it reflects the voice I have in my mind. It's unavoidable to be influenced by your favourite writers, especially early on, and that is just part of the learning process. Eventually, though, you'll find your own style and way of writing. Just write in a way that comes naturally to you. It will refine and develop as time goes by, and your body of work expands. The notebooks I have are a representation of just how much writing I have done. Each notebook is roughly 200 pages, but they are not the only place I journal. Periodically, I choose to write in Word documents or online at 750words, an online journaling tool. Is there any truth in the idea that you need to do 10,000 hours of something to master it? Or, in the case of writing, do you have to write thousands of words to become a good writer?

The truth is that you are a writer once you are writing. Once you commit to sitting down each day, or most days, and just write. Yet the answer is a little more complex—writing also requires editing, knowing what to get rid of, how to make a bad first draft shine (all first drafts are bad, even those by published authors), knowing the difference between plot and story, and reading as much as you possibly can. Reading as a writer also isn't as straightforward as just reading—sometimes you will need to think actively about what an author is doing, and how they are doing it. To try and understand the nuts and bolts of their writing and their style. Not to copy it, but to get a feel for craft, for how you use different tools to write a story or a non-fiction piece. There is a certain amount of truth to the idea that you need to write and edit thousands of words before you fully understand your craft, and even then, it may take a lifetime to master it. I've written thousands of words, and edited them, but I still feel like a beginner in many ways. I don't think that feeling will ever truly go away: every piece of writing I start work on is something new. Coming to the blank page is a new beginning every time.

I find it reassuring that even veteran writers have that same feeling—that each new piece of work is a blank canvas. That the struggle is that you have to move past the fear that you can't write, despite evidence to the contrary. Self-doubt is common, simply because writing is a leap of faith: faith that you intuitively know how to string a sentence together, that you understand story and the ideas you're trying to convey, and whether or not what you are writing is any good, there is bound to be a spark. Even if you don't write something you feel is great, or at least passable, your task is to understand what it takes to edit, re-write, and come closer to what you have in your mind. This is why I wrote 100,000 words of two novels I'm unlikely to ever publish, because the novel I'm working on now is a better, more coherent version of those two unfinished drafts. It made me understand that good writing takes its time, and there is no point in rushing a good story.

So why did I choose to write? Why didn't I decide on a less difficult, more financially stable calling? Most writers write because they can't not write, and because even on the bad days, they love words and language. I want to share that love of language, and how it is possible to convey ideas and images in word form. Nevertheless, writing is also an essential form of self-expression, a way to release difficult feelings and to make sense of your inner life, or the world around you. This is why, when I've left it days without writing, I feel congested, stressed, and on edge. For people with a tendency to ruminate and become anxious, writing can break that cycle, and become an invaluable way of processing your thoughts, a means of breaking the cycle. Writing is a gateway into understanding yourself better, being more self-aware, and hopefully leading into greater awareness of the inner lives and complexity of the people around you. When deeply into the flow of writing, it is as if the world falls away, and you become pure thought and feeling, with only the movement of your hand across the paper or your fingers on the keyboard. It's the kind of focus that we need in a world of digital distractions.

If you want to write, begin with a journal. Just use it to write whatever you want to write—use it for ideas, releasing your thoughts, poetry, quotes from other people, diary entries, phrases, writing about what you've seen, read, experienced. It began for me with picking up a notebook, and it will likely end, one day, with a few shelves of notebooks from years of writing. It's the one constant habit I've kept even when I've felt like giving up, and I feel that keeping a journal, a writer's notebook, can be the backbone to any writing practice. It will teach you to anchor yourself even when you have no time to do any other writing. Carry it with you everywhere, when you can. It's a physical manifestation of your commitment to writing. It will be the place you discover your voice, over months and years of just writing unselfconsciously, without any audience except yourself. When I first began journaling, I imagined that someone would see those words someday—some distant relative coming across a crate of notebooks—but I've let go of that fancy because writing in these journals is often repetitive, banal, and a place to lay down my cares. My other writing—essays, blog posts, poems, fiction—is the work that I do for public consumption. Journaling and writer notebooks are the scaffolding, the behind-the-scenes construction.

You don't have to keep a journal to be a writer, however. Many writing guides suggest that you start a 'writer's notebook' but if that doesn't work for you, there is no reason why you have to stick to it. Most of all, writing in a journal is good to empty your mind and ready it for the work ahead. Journaling itself is a good mindfulness practice, a good way to get used to sitting yourself down and focusing. It doesn't always work for everyone to keep a specific writer's notebook, and you don't have to write every day to be a good writer. It helps, to keep your brain used to the practice of writing, but it isn't essential. What matters is your commitment, writing when you can, as often as you can.

Whatever kind of writing you choose to do, it is all valid. It might take some time to find your way, because writing is something that needs practice—that is why it's called 'writing practice' and the 'writing craft'. The toolbox you need is something that can be learnt, that you can get better at. In the same way that an artist can learn a new technique, and then break all the rules, that is what you learn as a writer too. That learning never completely ends; writing needs constant work in order to become more intuitive, for you to understand where your weak points are, and what can be improved upon. The good news is that there are many good books on the writing craft, on how to cultivate the state of mind you need to see a piece of work through, and how to publish your book if you're an indie writer. At the end of this book, I've included a list of my favourite books for writers.

I consider writing one of my forms of activism and resistance. Writing, thinking critically, supporting activists, reading as much as I can, and sharing alternative ideas about life are the biggest tools I have to contribute to society. Some people are excellent at leading large groups of people or public speaking, whilst I have always found it easier to express myself in writing, to say what I need and want to say fluently. Resistance, for me, comes in the form of accepting and learning to love the body I live in, from not accepting the status quo that conflates self-worth with body size, it comes in the form of living and writing as a deaf person, and as a woman, of being brave and challenging myself to share writing about mental health, feminism, body positivity, and living as a highly sensitive, introverted person. I'm aware that the society I live in looks at someone like myself as marginal. Resistance is a fact of living in this body of mine, and writing is the way that I express that, is the way in which I push against social ostracization. I understand the privilege I have—I'm white, I've had a university education, I may be money-poor but lucky enough to have a supportive husband and parents, who allow me to live under their roof as a housemate. What I choose to do with this privilege—to support people who have even less of a chance to be heard—is hopefully a way of balancing some disparities and making a change.

So, writing can be a form of resistance. For some people who are living in a society where free-speech is enough for imprisonment, where you have to toe the status-quo and it is dangerous if you are writing (even reading) something different, it is an even bigger mark of resistance. Writing and free-speech go hand in hand as something that we must never take for granted, not in this time of political upheaval, media bias, and uncertainty. I feel that every piece of writing that is published (independently, traditionally, on blogs) is another day we get to resist and use our voices as a force for good. Finding your voice is an important rite of passage, and using your voice and platform for change is not a drop in the ocean—if enough people feel and think similarly, change is possible.

Then—write. Writing isn't elitist or just for people who want to be published writers. It's a way to understand yourself and the world better. It can improve mental health, help to heal you from past hurts and difficulties, and can be a way of expressing yourself when you need to. Nobody needs to see what you write if you prefer it to be that way. I've written thousands of words that nobody will ever get to see, and they have pulled me through periods of grief, depression, and personal crises. You will find yourself through years of writing, and see how you have changed as a person. If you do choose to share your writing, you will join people from all over the world, part of a tradition that includes diverse voices from across this planet of ours.

Choosing Encouragement

Everybody needs a champion, someone who encourages you and brings out the best in you. Whether this is actually someone else, or a voice in your head that spurs you onwards, doesn't matter. What does matter is that you understand that you are worth encouraging, that the work you are doing makes a difference, even if that is only to one person.

I'd be lying if I said that I don't write for anyone but myself. I used to believe that, but blogging helped me to understand that I do write for an audience—I do write to help, encourage, and let other people know they are not alone. I also write to entertain, to make people think, to inform and to share. We don't write into a vacuum. And yet I would still write without an audience.

When I first started keeping a writer's journal or notebook, I imagined someone, far into the future, finding a cache of dusty old journals and being inspired (or, equally, horrified) by what I was writing. Something shifted later on, though, as the lines became more clearly demarcated between the private thoughts, rough poetry, and problem solving of a journal, and the public, more filtered writing I share, through essays, blog posts, and fiction. I have an audience, and I wouldn't want to share the rough, unfinished writing in my notebooks. They're a testing ground.

Looking back on some of my journal entries, I can see that even in my darkest, most difficult moments, I always eventually come out through the other side, pushing and encouraging myself to see the good, the gratitude, the joy, the small pleasures and triumphs of life. Where does this small, self-assured and encouraging voice come from? From a deeper part of myself, that bypasses all the neuroticism and anxiety. It knows. It knows that no matter what I'm struggling with, no matter how difficult life is, I will learn something, I will be braver and stronger, and that there is so much beauty in life to appreciate.

This voice gives me far more strength and confidence than anything else. Outwardly, I struggle through, doubt myself, and speak in absolutes—'everything's going wrong!', 'I can't do this', 'who am I to think I could even try this?'—but that voice says 'Why not? You've done harder things before. Everything seems hard now, but it will feel good when it's done.' Having a part of yourself that trusts you to try, that knows what you're capable of, and that you have more strength than you give yourself credit for, has pulled me through the depths of grief and the murk of depression. You survive, you learn, and somewhere, deep inside, you take note and remember how strong you can be.

At the same time, we also need other people. To say otherwise is to underestimate the power of connection. We don't need other people to give us an ego boost (though occasionally, this can be rather nice), but we need other people's wisdom, and to be inspired. Encouragement doesn't have to be a straightforward 'you can do it! I believe in you!'—it can also come from your favourite writers, your favourite characters, other writers just like you, who have blogs and chat on Twitter.

There are two people I follow who are as different as night and day in their style of advice and encouragement to fellow authors and writers—Ksenia Anske, and Chuck Wendig. I started reading their blogs a number of years ago, just as Ksenia was self-publishing her first novels, *The Siren Suicides*, and just as Chuck released one of his first books of advice to writers, *Confessions of a Freelance Penmonkey*.

Ksenia's advice is nurturing, kind, full of enthusiasm and love, with her own dark Russian sense of humour. Chuck's is irreverent, often laced with imaginative expletives, pushy and funny. Both of them are important to me, representing two different kinds of encouragement. They are both champions of writers, whether self-published, conventionally published, beginner writers, or still writing their first book.

The best thing any writer can do is choose their favourite encouragers. Only you know what you need. Do you need expletive-laden tough love? Do you need gentle, kind, and nurturing word-hugs? Do you have favourite authors who have wonderful nuggets of wisdom about writing, and who will serve as guides when you hit a low point, or when you want some ideas? Mine your favourite novels and authors. Give yourself some time to look closely at what they do well, and how they did it. It will encourage you. It will give you what you need to keep going. Writers want each other to do well—at least the good ones do. I want other writers to write, and do their thing. We're keeping a tradition going that has lasted thousands of years: the art of telling a story, and sharing our ideas and opinions.

You may also be lucky enough to have a couple (or more) people in your life who believe in you and what you are doing. My sister gives me some ideas, and tells me to go write them. She made the suggestion that I write this book of essays. She knows I can do it, and having that belief and encouragement makes me feel ten feet tall on days when I'm in danger of tripping over my own fear. My husband has always supported me even when life has thrown us in the deep end. This is also why having a blog is a good idea. You comment on other people's blogs. They comment on yours. You encourage each other. You give love and receive love. Even with the existence of cyber-harassment and bullying, there are always chinks of light and love. Seek your community, and you'll find it.

I regularly search for books written about writing: I have my favourites. To begin with, it was Natalie Goldberg, author of *Writing Down the Bones*. Her style is deep, spiritual, searching, and kind. She makes the connection between meditation and writing, how when we are deeply focused on the page, our breathing evens, we relax, we are alert and alive, yet within a place of flow. She introduced me to the concept of 'monkey-mind'—the mind that bounces and procrastinates, restless, which would rather be doing anything else than writing.

My current mentor is Dani Shapiro, author of *Still Writing: The Perils and Pleasures of a Creative Life*, which is full of gems, ah-ha! moments, and a deep understanding of the encouragement that all writers need. She tells us that we need to be kind to ourselves, that we are undertaking a hard craft, constantly examining ourselves and scrutinising humanity and life. We ask big questions—of ourselves and others—and such intense scrutiny also needs to be balanced with kindness and gentle understanding. I'm guilty of burning myself out, of criticising myself for not getting as much done as I wanted to; when all I need, at times, is to breathe, take a step back, and look after myself.

In the end, we all need encouragement, whether we are writers, or simply trying to live and survive. Encouragement is the balm in a world that makes us feel insignificant and small, that runs on a treadmill of time and information. Seek out the people who encourage you, and encourage them in turn. Give yourself a chance to build up an inner voice that will always be there when you need it to be, that will guide you through your hardest, most despairing moments. Make it strong, and make it brave. Be your own champion, for the moments when no-one else can.

Energy

Filling yourself up, breathing life into yourself, is now harder than it has ever been. We live in a twenty-four-seven connected world of information, a superhighway of streams and channels. We connect with other people over shared interests, the same causes, our blogs, Twitter, Instagram, and Facebook. There is no escaping it—even when we are switched off, we feel that urgency, the noise, encroaching on time that we used to take for granted.

Boredom is one of the biggest issues of our time. We don't get bored, because we have so many shiny, bright lures calling our name. We can play games, comment on blogs, watch Netflix, read articles, pin on Pinterest, endlessly scroll through everything. Why is boredom important? Because it tells us what we truly want to be doing. Instead, we distract ourselves, take the easiest option available. I'm certainly guilty of reaching for my phone when I could do something else, something that requires more effort, but would be more rewarding and satisfying. We make choices each day about where to spend our energy. Yet energy isn't infinite—humans don't have as much energy as we'd like to have. Brain power deteriorates over the course of a day, as we get tired and slide into decision fatigue.

Taking steps to whittle apps and intrusions down to the bare minimum works to an extent. My experiments—removing

Facebook from my phone, using Pocket to save interesting articles instead of reading them right away, sticking my phone on airplane mode when I don't want the temptation—sometimes work, sometimes don't. More often than not, I find myself instead accessing Facebook through my browser, checking Instagram, and actually getting distracted and searching for articles to add to Pocket, instead of working on my own articles.

When you're self-employed, it is especially hard to maintain the discipline to resist distraction. You'll find that occasionally events and people will distract you, which is fine, but the difference with how technology has progressed is that it's made it harder to focus. Intense bursts of energy and focus are how tasks get done—not multi-tasking, and having broken attention. One thing at a time, doing a job well, is what it takes. Despite knowing this, I find my attention over the years has become scattered, fragmented, and I am far more restless and prone to sailing off-course.

You may think that introverts don't worry about connecting with others, or keeping up with friends. That couldn't be further from the truth. As I mentioned in the article 'On Introversion', the most widely accepted definition of introversion is that we are more easily stimulated—that we can deal with social interaction for a certain period of time before we run out of energy and need to recharge in solitude, or at least with quiet, reflective time. Introverts have also found that socialising online has been a life-saver: they get to know people well, far more in-depth than just through face to face interaction. But too much of this, too, can drain energy. Keeping that in mind, it's no wonder that if we spend too much time on Facebook or Twitter, thinking about and interacting with others, we will become fatigued and run out of precious energy.

This is why energy is such an important thing to guard—for everyone. We are better at being human when we choose more carefully what we spend our time doing, where we put our attention. I've been careless in the past—giving all my energy to others and having none left over for myself and my own projects—so I have been learning to choose more carefully. I take the time to decide each morning or at the beginning of a week what my biggest priorities are, and what the less important ones are. If I get the bigger ones prioritised, I can then deal with the other tasks and activities. I'm learning, though, that if I want to have that all-important energy, I have to constantly maintain a balance between everything. In its own way, that can be hard work. My brain is a constant juggling act of keeping many balls in the air. This is why prioritising and doing at least one thing a day to further a goal is important. Otherwise I would be trying to do it all at once, snatching at one ball, then another, in a flurry of panicked activity.

For writers, especially, it's important to understand your own energy and how to direct it. It might seem boring to other people, disciplining yourself to sit down each day and write, doing the hard work of pulling words out of your head. You may have to turn social engagements down, or work into the night, or get up at the crack of dawn before the rest of the house is awake. To write is to direct your energy into daydreaming, thinking, planning, sitting down and typing or scratching a pen on paper. It's an internal process, one in which our energy is alive and observant, but also looking into your own internal world and emotions. You have to be happy with some kind of solitude. You won't always be alone when you write—if you favour cafés for example, or work in a studio with other people—but the fundamental condition of writing is being alone, shining a torch into your own dark psyche.

You also direct your attention and energy into what inspires you, what gives you ideas. Reading, watching films, going on walks to observe the world and think, constantly accumulating quotes and words, sharpening your curiosity, seeing art, making art, listening to and observing other people, learning about random topics as diverse as the cosmos and how the underground system works. This is what we have to do to fill ourselves up. This is why Pocket works for me—

I grab at all the information I can find, store it somewhere safe until I'm ready to fill up on ideas. Perhaps this is why we shouldn't be so hard on ourselves too—technology is a beautiful thing when it does what it should be doing, and connects us to each other, and with other ideas. It is when we tip over too far, stray from the place we need to be to keep our balance that it begins to unravel.

Slipping into that place of focused energy is hard, at first. Every time I show up at my desk, I struggle. I feel the urge to check Instagram bubble up. I think I should check the calendar to see if everything has been included. I wonder if I should find out if a friend wants to meet up. Or if the weather is going to be good for the rest of this week. I resist. I open up my notebook and write some bad poetry. I turn on my laptop. I focus my energy on opening Word, writing a first sentence, then another, until a whole paragraph appears like magic. I get distracted by the sound of shutters banging on the window in the wind. My eye is dragged to the music playing on my phone. My hand reaches across, but at the last minute I redirect that movement to reaching for my tea. It's a dance, a dance of resistance, redirecting, focusing. Eventually, your mind gets used to this space of quiet and energy, and even begins to joyfully, quietly, long for it.

Poetry Resurgence

Poetry is often seen as being too 'establishment' or otherwise inaccessible. Unless they are poems for children, lyrics, or haiku, easy to digest and remember. The forms seem impenetrable, the references too out of reach, unless you are willing to put the research in to pull the poem apart. Maybe we think all poems should rhyme, or that the ones that don't rhyme belong to 'Instagram' poets, perhaps a little too twee and cliched, words that wouldn't be out of place in a Hallmark card.

I started writing lyrics when I was fifteen, a time when I was going through various emotional upheavals and a severe bout of undiagnosed anxiety. It gave me an outlet to express my feelings— from anger to longing—and helped me to process the confusion of the teenage years. These were the kind of lyrics with a chorus, plenty of rhyming, and full of metaphors inspired by indie and rock music. I wasn't a big reader of poetry, since the poetry I was exposed to were mainly dead white men, writing about love, war, and daffodils—not that they weren't beautiful or haunting, just that I couldn't relate to them. Later on, when I reached my A Levels, I was exposed to Carol Ann Duffy and John Keats, which more than made up for it. Though Keats is one of those 'classic' poetry writers, his poems are infused with passion, wonder, and an appreciation for life. Carol Ann Duffy writes poems that deal with human emotions, situations, and even, in her *The World's Wife* (and later, *Feminine Gospels*) themes of feminism, power dynamics, and the supernatural. They were my first major introduction to the power of good poetry.

Fast forward to 2015, the year I read Nikita Gill's poetry on Pinterest, and fell in love with her way of describing emotion through the cosmos, stars, and nature. It was Pinterest that revived my interest in writing and reading poetry. Taking photos of written or typed poems, turning words into works of art, drove a resurgence of poetry. From Nikita Gill, I discovered Rupi Kaur, Nayyirah Waheed, Victoria Erickson, and Mary Oliver. All of them use words to describe moments, emotions, nature, life, and experience, in beautiful, profound ways. It made me excited about writing and reading poetry again.

Before all this, I occasionally wrote poems in my writer's notebooks, again mostly connected with a desire to express certain feelings, to work something out, to capture moments that didn't make sense to me. They were private, not meant for sharing. I didn't have the confidence or the self-assurance to be able to share poems when I didn't consider myself a 'poet' in the traditional sense of the word. My poems seemed small, half-formed, lacking any kind of formal structure other than occasional verses or rhyme schemes. Poetry was the domain of those who knew more about poetry structure and rhyme than I did. Or at least I thought it was.

I attempted traditional forms of poems when I did a course in Creative Writing with the Open University. It introduced me to the concept of free-verse, prose poems, and contemporary poetry. In many ways, poems are organic, intuitive forms—they find their own structure, one that feels right when you are writing the poem itself. It can be anything from a couple of lines, to an epic poem with a narrative. Just like fiction writing and essay writing, a structure emerges when you're writing. Though my personal poems didn't appear to have any clear structure, they were still organised into verses of four to six lines, some with alternate line verses, some without rhyme at all.

With poetry, I feel that confidence comes with finding something that works for you. Poems are small slices of meaning and metaphor, a micro version of a story, or a photograph in words. Confidence grows when you write enough poems that your own voice emerges, one that feels natural and unforced. They explore emotions, situations, and topics that preoccupy you, what you have learnt, observed, felt. They are good places to play with words, to find the exact right word for something, to dig into language.

This is why the poetry community on Instagram is so important, despite the critics. It's a way for people to find their voices, to play with language, and express what is otherwise hard to express. It's a combination of words and image, an interplay between the visual and written metaphor. Like I did, you often have to write a whole lot of bad poetry to find your voice and to improve your writing. Writing is a craft like any other—you work at it, study language, discover your own voice and interests, and produce a volume of work—some good, some bad, some terrible, and some with flashes of brilliance.

Most of my poems are always altered from the first draft. The first draft always includes a vagueness, that needs sharpening and defining. Words that don't belong, or words that don't make sense. Or there may need to be another verse, something to make the poem sing. The great thing about poems is that they are generally small, and you can play around with synonyms, finding the exact word. Lately, my poems have been about mental health, personal growth, and the condition of the planet and humanity, what matters to me.

I took part in a 100 day project on Instagram where I wrote 100 poems—matching them to images from an attribution-free website. It was a way for me to develop my voice and style, to find a way of expressing myself with the least amount of words. It feeds into the rest of my writing, helping me to be more economical, a little more thoughtful about what words I use. I believe that all writers should try writing poetry, because whether or not you choose to share it, it is a great way to hone your voice, to use language in a finer way.

Most important, though, I believe poetry should be accessible, and the tools to decipher more structured, classic poetry should also be accessible. Simply because poetry is the form of writing that speaks to our human hearts. Not all poetry appeals to everyone, but no doubt there is a poet, or a poem, out there for everybody, just as I believe there is a book out there for everyone. Poetry is bottled emotion, as powerful as someone saying 'I understand, this is what it feels like'—and handing you the key to understanding your own heart. When you most need it, poetry can console you, can make you laugh, can make you nod your head in recognition. Just like the lyrics to your favourite song—a poem can last a lifetime.

Why Genre Matters

When it comes to genre, there is this assumption within the literary industry, and amongst some readers, that genre reads are less worthy and complex than so-called literary fiction. As a long-time reader of books that can be placed squarely within genre fiction—such as paranormal fantasy, straight fantasy, horror, urban fantasy, and forays into crime and thriller—this assumption doesn't chime with my experience. Some of the books I read, too, have been tarred with the so-called 'chick-lit' label, which has been both insulting and a great disservice to the authors, not to mention dismissive of women writers as a whole. I believe that any reading is good—that we shouldn't have any guilt about what we choose to read.

'Literary fiction' itself is a peculiar label. The books I have read within this category have included everything from character-driven novels to books with an element of magical realism or fantasy. The distinction appears to be that books within genre writing follow a particular formula or have certain 'rules' that readers recognise, and are comfortable with, whilst literary fiction can be experimental, dealing with subjects that have 'literary merit', such as political criticism and social commentary, or a focus on the human condition.

Nevertheless, many of my favourite writers within genre fiction also focus on political, social, and human concerns. Ursula K. Le Guin, for example, has written complex, gender-bending novels within the science fiction and fantasy genre, such as *The Dispossessed* and *The Left Hand of Darkness*. Marge Piercy's *Woman on the Edge of Time* and *He, She, and It* are both examples of powerful works of social and political fiction squarely within the science fiction and dystopian genre, as is Margaret Atwood's *The Handmaid's Tale*, more widely recognised as a masterpiece.

These novels are part of feminist science fiction writing, which arguably began with Mary Shelley's *Frankenstein*. Science fiction writing done well can be a conduit to exploring themes that might be awkward within a book that lacks exploration of other worlds and alien cultures, time travel and future Earth, of the possibility of science changing the way we relate to each other, and how the human body and psyche could evolve. Imaginary possibilities allow us to look at our current systems and cultures through a different lens.

Within paranormal urban fantasy, too, I have found characters who, as well as battling all manner of supernatural forces, also deal with misogyny and sexism. Urban fantasy, particularly written by women authors, has a reputation for strong female characters with plenty of attitude. Though for many books this is true, I have also found that the best authors know when to test their characters, when to show vulnerability and team-work, and how to develop and grow their characters. Kelley Armstrong's *Women of the Otherworld* books are a wonderful example of a series of books that deserve greater recognition and readership, as well as Kim Harrison's *The Hollows* series. At first glance, you might consider them to be typical commercial supernatural fiction, but as someone who has read a lot of urban fantasy, this is a genre that deserves to be recognised as a place where there are some incredible characters and storylines.

What captures my attention with particular books within genres tends to be subject and world-building, as well as compelling characters. To build intricate rules and structures, yet with a lightness of touch, within a fantasy or science fiction world takes time and effort. To imagine cultures which contrast or re-imagine our own, and to bring to life the people within those cultures, to keep track of them throughout a novel or a series of novels takes discipline. We only have to think of J.K. Rowling and her sprawling notes on plot and world-building to understand the time and effort that goes into fantasy and science-fiction writing. Even within Tolkien's work there is social and political commentary, though it is not immediately obvious.

It does all readers and authors a disservice to assume that there is no intelligence or power within the writing in commercial genres. If that were the case, these genres would die out, and we wouldn't have the successes of *Game of Thrones*, *Harry Potter*, or even *Sherlock*. Genre is popular for a reason—because it is the perfect fusion of action, plot, and thoughtful, often intelligent treatment of character and social or political subjects. Even some Marvel films look closely at character and social commentary, at political commentary— because not to do so would relegate these films to mindless superhero action. To be dismissive of genre as samey and pointless is to sneer at the power of the human imagination.

It's no secret that one of my favourite authors is Jane Austen, and she provides an interesting case-study into what happens when 'genre' is applied to someone's writing. Many people consider Austen's work to be so-called 'chick-lit' which, whilst a derogatory and undermining term for commercial women's fiction, is universally recognised. Austen's work, for those who haven't read it, has generally been categorised as period romance, as women's fiction.

Still, she can be found in various genres and categories. Her work can be classified as period social commentary, period satirical works, character-led novels, classics, and yes, even literary fiction. If we take a closer look at the elements of her novels, which include social commentary, are character-driven, include subtle satirical elements, and strong character development, we can conclude that there is a case to be made for placing her within literary fiction. What could this mean for other books which are placed within so-called women's commercial fiction? How often are books written by women relegated to this genre, or dismissed by readers and publishers?

For the most part, genre is basically a way for booksellers and publishers to separate books into categories for selling. It makes it easier for readers to browse books online and in bookshops, rather than having to trawl through everything to find something they might like. There is a case to be made that we are missing out by not considering reading outside our comfort zones. Or believing that only literary fiction is worthy of literary prizes and plaudits. If you take away genre, you are left with story, with character, with ideas and imaginary leaps. I used to feel some element of shame that I love to read genre books, but why should we be ashamed to love what we love, when it so obviously enhances our lives? By all means, read everything, read as much as you can for as long as you are here.

Creative Pursuits

Children have a naturally curious and playful nature, that leads them to put their energy into creating, exploring, noticing what adults don't, and asking questions that we often don't know how to answer. When my sister Sarah was little, she would ask 'why?' so often, that I often made up the answers. Children don't care about making a mess, or being perfect, and will leap both hands in, smearing paint or food all over themselves.

As adults, after being schooled, and after going into the world of work, sometimes we lose this capacity for play, for allowing messiness and being messy, caring too much about perfection, and not asking enough questions. We lose our sense of wonder at the world around us because everything becomes familiar and named. We stop thinking about the processes, about the inner workings of something, and sometimes, we forget to look up or down at the wonder of the earth and sky.

When we got married, Dan and I decided to craft and DIY a number of our wedding decorations as well as design our invitations, wedding programs, place-settings, and table-plan. This was a year of intense crafting and creating where we roped in family to help, and even had a couple of projects we were working on the night before the wedding itself. In the end, even though the ring-box was half finished and we didn't have enough helium to fill the three giant balloons, there was an immense sense of accomplishment. We built three papier-mâché floor sculptures of books, countless paper roses for the backs of the chairs, and used plenty of glue. Mostly though, it rekindled a desire to invent, and an enthusiasm for working with our hands.

It took me another year and a half before I took up that enthusiasm fully. After the builders had put up the studio in the garden, Sarah, myself, and our parents worked hard to paint the inside and outside of the studio, painted a couple of old pieces of furniture with chalk paint, and created a space where we would work—and play. The studio is far more than a workspace. We used the money we inherited from Auntie Marjorie, Granny's cousin, to create a space that reminds us of people no longer with us, of their encouragement and love. A space where the past intersects with the present. It's a place of promise and of hope and has acted as a place to go when in need of calm and relaxation.

Once everything was assembled, I spent a year writing this book of essays; but also, a year taking up and trying various creative pursuits. Those pursuits allowed me to work through a number of difficult emotions and situations, helped me to become more mindful, and enabled me to practice the long periods of absorption and focus I needed for my writing. It's not easy in this day and age to avoid the lure of social networking and scrolling, and keep away from instant socialising, so I needed the practice and mental space created by these moments of creativity. Slow creative practices are a respite from anxiety and stress present in so much of modern life and work.

For example, I took up cross-stitching. I began with a cross-stitch kit I bought from Etsy, and by the time the studio was done, I had finished. It was something that took concentration and focus, and couldn't be finished in one quick hour. It opened me up to trying other needlecraft styles, varying in complexity and dedication. I had always been in awe of Granny's embroidery pictures, one of which now hangs in the hall at home; I had always wanted to try embroidery myself but didn't know where to start. Cross-stitching is a great place to begin—all you need is Aida fabric, a needle, scissors, a cross-stitch hoop, a pattern, and a collection of cotton threads.

The great news about cross-stitching is that there has never been such a variety of fun, modern, and inspirational patterns available as there are now. If you want to stitch quotes from your favourite films or books, you can. If you want to stitch a portrait of yourself and your family, or you and your cat (or dog), you can either illustrate something yourself or find someone who can, then convert it to a cross-stitch pattern online (much easier than it sounds)—or even convert a photo to a cross-stitch pattern. There are plenty of new and old books full of cross-stitch patterns. Even men are getting into it, with people like Mr X Stitch, Jamie Chalmers, creating designs that everyone will love.

I'm a great believer in taking up hobbies, and particularly meaningful hobbies. Hobbies that have a meaning for you, whether because they connect you to a sense of childlike play, or because they remind you of someone, or a good time in your life. You might think of hobbies as relics of the past, what people used to do because they had the time, in sheds at the back of the garden. But it's never been easier or more exciting to take up new interests—because there is a whole community out there doing the same thing. On Instagram, I find inspiration from other cross-stitchers and embroiderers, and find new places to buy patterns. Youtube and Pinterest are great places for inspiration and tutorials, for everything from embroidery to building robots.

In his book *Rest: Why You Get More Done When You Work Less*, Alex Soojung-Kim Pang writes about the importance of 'deep play' to a life well lived. Deep play is essentially an activity that is meaningful, that uses skills you have in a different way to how you use them at work, and is deeply restorative to your mind. These activities allow you to learn more about something, perhaps to innovate, and use your mind and body differently than you usually do in everyday life. I find activities that are more manual (such as cross-stitching, DSLR photography, painting, collaging, and hand-lettering), allow me to move away from the intense work of writing. I find meaning in these activities because they allow me to make sense of or celebrate what matters to me, and to develop my spatial skills, as well as my eye for photography. Even cooking gives me a chance to shift gears and use different creative skills.

Even if you don't think of yourself as creative, you may not be thinking of the many creative tasks you do on a daily basis. We are consistently making decisions, such as what to wear and what to eat (or cook), relaying stories in conversation, daydreaming, and various other mental and physical activities in the course of a day. Everything we use and see was once the daydream or invention of another human being—we are surrounded by creativity everywhere we go—and it only takes a shift in mindset to acknowledge that as a species, we are constantly creative. We don't have to make grand works of art. Neither do you have to be some kind of genius, or suffer for your art, or allow it to become another pressure in your life. Creativity, even when you have to work at it, should be at least a little bit joyful, at least a tiny bit fun.

This is why, if you are prone to being a perfectionist, taking up a hobby is such a good idea. If you let go of the idea that everything has to be perfect, always done to your best, highest standards, then hobbies give you a respite from that. Over time, you get better and learn new skills, but to begin with, they remind us that we're beginners, and that we have to learn and pay attention to improve. Messiness is a bonus—the messier a hobby is, the better. I often find stray threads of cotton hanging out on my clothes, or splashes of paint on my desk.

Often, pursuing creative activities allows us to ask questions that we don't know the answer to, and to seek out the answers. When I started cross-stitching, I didn't know anything much about sewing, or material. Trying new creative challenges makes you braver and more curious: it leads you to try other related activities, or even pursue interests completely unrelated to the task in question. I've learnt more about the history of stitching, and how it has been used by women to protest for suffrage, for example. It led me towards learning about craftivism, and how we can use crafts in our activism. If you leap in with an open mind, you will learn more about yourself and the world around you—and beyond your own experience.

In the end, creativity is whatever you want it to be. It can be telling stories, cooking, learning an instrument, dancing, singing, writing songs, building structures, putting together and making cosplay outfits, stitching, or drawing. It can be a part of your everyday life, sitting alongside you on your daily commute, and when you play with your children, talk to your friends, and sing in the shower. Creativity gives us hope and improves our wellbeing, when life is uncertain or difficult, and can be a source of great happiness.

Blogging, A Universe

Blogging, first coined as a term in 1997 by Jorn Barger as a way to describe logging his internet activity, is a ubiquitous and accessible way for people to find an audience for their writing. Originally, blogging was much like a personal diary, a way for people to share their observations, thoughts, and photos. These days, blogs can be anything from political opinion and reporting, to a Mum blogging her way through parenthood. Communities have sprung up around blogging, and many bloggers have made a career through their sites. The possibilities for blogs these days is almost limitless.

I started blogging as an experiment, back in 2005, after Dan introduced me to blogspot.com. To begin with, I used it much like a diary: posting my thoughts, writing about university, sharing my poems and lyrics. A year later, it transitioned into a feminist blog, as I discovered the fledgling feminist online community. A few major implosions and blog-wars later, after moving said feminist blog over to Wordpress.com, I upped sticks altogether to my current blog, *Cats and Chocolate*, tired of the same old in-fighting and misunderstandings. I've been blogging for twelve years and *Cats and Chocolate* has been my online home for at least ten of those years: I've travelled from the early days of diary blog posts towards a blog that has grown and changed as I have grown and changed.

Along the way, I've tried many experiments—some successful,

and others less so. For a little while, I had another blog specifically for plus size fashion and body-acceptance blogging, but eventually decided to close that down too, because I felt it was going too much towards consumerism, unsustainable for me in the long term, and felt I had lost my original aims of challenging norms of beauty, and celebrating different body types. The community, however, was lovely, and I still try to keep up as much as I can with some people I met along the way. The same can be said of the feminist blogging community—I met some wonderful people, and in some respects, this is what has kept me from giving up on blogging altogether.

The heartening thing about blogging is that anyone can do it. It is, or should be, a level playing field. All you need is an internet connection, access to a computer, and a desire to share with other people. Or, at least, a desire to write into the void, regardless of who might be listening. It's an excellent means of testing and developing your writing voice, discovering it and being willing to work at it over the years. Though I look back and cringe a little at what I used to write about, those early blog posts are where I began to work on my craft and writing voice. They are where I found a place to be authentic, myself, without hiding what I was really excited about, what I loved, and what I wanted to do and be. Those young, first attempts at blogging are where I learnt to grow my wings, and learnt to be brave, less afraid of sharing.

There is some truth in the idea that to become good at something, you have to first put in 10,000 hours of practice, as suggested by Malcolm Gladwell in his book *Outliers*. Blogging is, and was, my 10,000 hours. Though it's debatable that 10,000 hours is necessary, the regular practice helped. The idea being that if you write as much as you can, you will begin to feel the effects of that writing, and will mature and learn to trust your instincts. I am more willing to be open-hearted and brave with my writing, even though sometimes, the truth is hard to write. Blogging has been a good companion in that respect because every time I click the 'publish' button, I'm scared, in that exhilarated, falling off a cliff kind of way. It pushes you to write the uncomfortable, real, and true things. Otherwise, we aren't going deep enough, and don't test ourselves.

As a testing ground, blogging also builds confidence. The comments and community that rise up from that sharing is one of the best outcomes, not only because of the positivity, but because you can see people reading your work, and treating it as real and valid. I believe that bloggers are writers. I feel that if you write, you are a writer, and blogging is writing. It takes effort and time to assemble a blog post—not just the writing, but coming up with a title, finding appropriate images (or taking your own photos or making your own art), using categories and tags, and using links to connect your posts to relevant articles or other blogs. It's a creative, and yet technical way to self-publish your work. You eventually learn discipline, and new skills, coming up with new ways to write and create.

For writers, who have traditionally been solitary creatures, being part of a wider community is priceless. The reason I love Wordpress is that the community is a network of spider webs, and everyone, in some way, is connected. The founders of Wordpress.com stand up for free-speech and protect that right to the best of their ability. They care about the community of bloggers hosted on their platform. I've been lucky enough to have a couple of my blog posts recognised with Freshly Pressed, a featured-post page which has now been changed to 'Discover', and I felt as though all those years of blogging had connected me with a huge, bright community of people. Some of those people have become friends, people I respect and admire. I feel lucky that I've been able to find those people, or that they have found me.

I'm not someone who feels that blogging itself should be picked up as a way to make money. It should always, I feel, begin because you want to do it, because you have something to say, and to share. It can be a way to connect to other writers, and to share your published work, but I'm a little wary of the idea that blogging itself should be monetised. At the same time, I understand that it can be used as a conduit, and set up as a website to sell your writing and creative work, as well as blogging. But if you don't love blogging and writing itself, there is little point starting one.

I struggled for a while with how to make money blogging, but I feel that it would take the joy out of it for me. I'm willing to use a platform such as Patreon, to set up pages on my blog for selling my published books, and links directing my readers to my articles or short stories, or information products (such as short e-courses), but I don't think I would add ads or banners. Unless they truly are products that I support, like other people's books or artwork. However, you can do this with blogs, and it's entirely up to the blogger what they feel they can gain from monetising. The point of blogging, for me, has always been to try and hone my writing, to share what I love, and to be part of a wider community.

What is the secret of blogging longevity? Above all, it's the ability to be flexible, to allow your blog to move with your changing interests and periods of life. I understand the idea of having a blogging niche. It makes it easier for people to categorise your blog and decide if they want to read it, easier for people to find you according to their interests. Given this, I don't know how I would categorise my blog. In the broadest terms, it may be a lifestyle blog, except it isn't, because I blog heavily about books and reading, except for when I'm writing about topics like depression, philosophy, empathy, and kindness. Or, even, reviewing films and TV series. My blog flows with what interests me, that concern me at any given moment, that I feel that other people might also find interesting. Perhaps you just need a hook or two to get people interested in what you're writing, and then allow them to explore the rest of the blog. You don't have to restrict yourself to being 'about' one particular thing.

As with all writing, you also need patience. I spent a number of years without a large volume of followers, and appreciated every comment I got (I still do). It is nice when you do eventually build up a following, but it's always the regular faces and commenters that make it worth it. So be patient—comment on other people's blogs, enjoy each new reader, be willing to keep writing even on the days when your blog stats tell you only one person has read your blog this week. It is at least one person—how incredible. The writing is the thing, in the beginning. If you want community, go find it, and send appreciation and love to other people's blogs. The world needs more of that anyway, and it always feels good to tell people you appreciate them and their work. It can often lead to lifelong friendships and the opportunity for creative collaboration.

Blogging is one of the best ways to start writing—it's easy to start, and you learn as you go along. I'm grateful that I started a blog all those years ago; without it I wouldn't have learnt the power of community, and it would have taken me much longer to hone my writing voice. Blogs show the power of the internet—the power of the individual voice, separate from corporations and governments. It gives you freedom to grow into the writer within.

Part Five:
Society and Identity

Sound Memories

I was six years old when my aunt noticed that I couldn't hear the telephone ringing. Until then, somehow, I had thrived. I held conversations with my grandparents whilst in the backseat of their car, without seeing their faces. I would come when people called me. My parents read books to me in bed, and I thought I could hear every word. I could watch films and understand the plot, or at least, at the time, it seemed that way.

I don't remember my first audiology appointment. They have all blurred into each other—the bleep tests, the headphones, the doctors, the waiting rooms, the tiredness and the desire to get home back to the familiar. In time, those waiting rooms themselves became familiar, the brown slippery leather seats, piles of colourful plastic toys on the ground, other kids and their restless parents. First, we would go to the audiology department to get an audiogram, measuring my hearing, and then we would go and wait to see the doctor.

I had a couple of doctors, but the one I remember most was Mr Martin. He was a kind and optimistic man, putting my parents at ease, who wanted the best for his young patients. He was tolerant of my restlessness, and encouraging of what I was interested in, like reading, art, crafts, and drama. In hindsight, having a doctor who was positive and optimistic shaped my attitude to my deafness. I never felt as if I was missing out, even when I had difficult days, simply because my parents were reassured, and never made me feel as though I couldn't do something.

The ear-mould impression fittings, at first bizarre and mildly uncomfortable, became my favourite part of audiology appointments. They would push a little foam piece attached to string into the ear canal, and put the string around the back of my ears. Then they would make up the white putty, adding a blue coloured activator from a tube to it, kneading both together, and syringe it into the ear, pressing it in a little afterwards. It was cold, and warmed up as the putty hardened. If I was lucky, they would give me the leftovers, which I could roll around in my hands to make a bouncy ball, whilst waiting for the impressions to set.

Now, as an adult, I still love the process. It's a strange, secret pleasure that many deaf people enjoy. Most deaf people I know have admitted, at one time or another, that getting ear-mould impressions is one of the best sensations ever. Not so much the ear-moulds themselves, which cause all kinds of issues, from itchy ears, eczema, cartilage rubbings, and ear-infections or aches. But if you want sound, the only other option is a cochlear implant, which solves the problem of ear-moulds, but are a permanent option needing thought, time, and assessment (not to mention an operation). Mr Martin felt that cochlear implantation was a decision for when I was older, when I understood the implications, and my parents felt the same.

In medical language, I was diagnosed with profound sensorineural progressive hearing loss. In lay terms, it means that I have hearing loss of more than 95 decibels (profound), that my hearing loss is due to damage or impaired function of the inner ear (sensorineural), and that my hearing could deteriorate over time, with small or large falls (progressive). My sister was also diagnosed with the same. The cause, we found, some years later, may have been something to do with the combination of my parent's DNA, in a way, a genetic cause. Though nobody in our family is completely deaf, at least not from genetic causes. Both our parents are hearing, and usually, deaf children are born to hearing families.

Humans are adaptable. Our senses compensate. We learn other ways of accessing the world, different ways, when we have an imbalance of senses. Those different ways allow us to work around perceived limitations, and barriers we come across. For deaf and hard of hearing people, the most profound barriers are around communication and the sound-dominated society we live in. Depending on clarity of hearing, your language (sign-language or English, or both), and your preferences, you will need some measure of technological or human adaptation, from sign-language interpreters, to speech to text (or captioning and subtitling), to lip-speakers.

Our eyes become our ears. Peripheral vision becomes more important. We lipread, take in visual cues, become highly attuned to what is going on around us, from body language and facial expressions, to the way a crowd is moving. Context becomes everything. You can't follow a conversation without understanding the context—the subject—that is being discussed. This is why context is so important when you're learning British Sign Language (BSL). I've tried, over the years, to follow conversations in hearing company, which can leap from one subject to another, missing the context, and becoming more than a little confused and frustrated. Fast moving banter is a no-go when you're a lip-reader, unless you know the lip-pattern so well that there is no danger of missing the context.

Then there's the light. Light is important. If someone is standing in front of a bright light, such as the sun or a lamp, their faces and bodies are cast into silhouette and you can't see their lips or their hands. Equally, people forgetting themselves and covering their face, chewing, turning away, and moving around, is another obstacle. Then there is the fatigue, which all deaf people and children may encounter, whether daily or after socialising. The concentration it takes for communication is draining—so don't be surprised if a deaf person becomes less patient, distracted, or more prone to mistakes when lipreading as the day wears on.

Since I'm someone who lip-reads and accesses the world through text and words, I rely on people being clear with communication, and on subtitles, captions and speech to text. I'm lucky that in the UK, most entertainment I consume is subtitled—Netflix, BBC and terrestrial channels, and most DVDs. There are also occasional showings of films with subtitles, though this has its issues. There is always a but: not everything is subtitled. Even some DVDs lack subtitling, which is more than a little disappointing, and it is only recently that Netflix and Amazon have upped their game and provided subtitling for the majority of their content. Cinemas can be notoriously inconsistent with communication across their employees when it comes to subtitled films—I've had many issues with turning up to a film and finding that we have to ask them to restart the film with subtitles, or even have to leave with a refund because they don't have the subtitle track. Despite all this, I've seen many wonderful films at the cinema because of subtitling, and don't take that for granted.

Most live events don't have subtitling. As much as I would like to attend as many writing conferences as I can, I would have to ask the organisers to provide access or pay for my own, which would be expensive. It means picking and choosing, and also sticking to events that are subtitled through Stagetext or speech to text reporting. I'm always happy when I get to access events that I wouldn't ordinarily be able to, like conferences and talks. My most recent experiences were seeing Caitlin Moran at the WOW (Women of the World) festival at the Southbank Centre in 2016, and Tom Hanks, talking about his new book of short stories in 2017. Pure joy.

My Mum is a theatre captioner, freelance for Stagetext and the RSC. Through her, I've been privileged to see many wonderful theatre shows over the years, from *Sweeney Todd* to *The Taming of the Shrew* at Shakespeare's Globe. This is how we have adapted as a family, and how my Mum has found her passion. Language surrounds us, clarifies the meaning of what we experience. You put context around being deaf, and try to make sense of it.

I have an auditory memory. The memory of sounds. I remember sounds and connect them to what I can still hear. All deaf people experience sound, or the absence of sound, differently. With my hearing aids, I still understand and can hear far more than most people expect me to. Music, and the timbre of voices, airplanes, the whir of a fan, the loud, insistent call of my cat when the room is quiet. The whine of car engines rushing by. The bellow of the wind. The crashing thunder of the sea. I know what birds are meant to sound like, but I can't hear them. It depends on my mood, but I'm rarely sad about that. I see them, in all their colours and grace. I'm secure in myself, in my status and fact of my deaf self. I hear what I hear, and I don't hear what I don't hear. Life goes on. My attitude is one of acceptance, and joy of what I do have. My eyes are hungry for the world, and for words, and language.

Cinema Blues

As I get older, my memory becomes fuzzy, faded like an old photograph, harder to see. Sensory memories are the strongest: the scent of Diorella or Chanel No. 5, both of which I associate with my Granny, the taste and scent of satsumas, getting glue on my hands and remembering countless craft sessions. In particular, scent, music (not necessarily 'sound'), sight, and taste have a firm hold upon what I remember. Films, such as *Star Wars*, conjure up scenes at my grandparent's bungalow, and certain films are firmly associated with my childhood, then my teenage years, and finally, adulthood.

Childhood films were both a joy and frustration. At the time, in the mid-to-late eighties and early nineties, films like *The Goonies*, Disney films, *The Neverending Story*, *Legend*, and *Willow*, were favourites—yet largely didn't have closed-captions or subtitles, which I would have needed in order to know what was being said (and follow the storylines). However, for whatever reason, I was happy to just sit and watch, whether or not subtitles were provided.

My hearing dropped a number of times later on, and perhaps I had just enough to get the gist of what was happening in the films I was watching. The dialogue and storylines became much clearer to me in the mid-nineties, when closed-captioning and Ceefax became available. This exploded my world further – I was completely enthralled with films. This was a great time for people who love cinema—*Jurassic Park*, *Die Hard*, *Blade Runner*, *Four Weddings and a Funeral*, *Alien*, *Practical Magic*—some extraordinary films and TV series came out. It also gave me the opportunity to watch old favourites with subtitles, which was when I became aware of the language in *The Goonies* (hilarious), the lyrics to *The Neverending Story* theme, and of course, the endlessly quotable dialogue in *Star Wars*.

By the time I was at secondary school, I was spoilt for choice with series like *Buffy The Vampire Slayer* generally being consistently subtitled on TV. However, the cinema situation was, and still is, awkward, often disappointing, and still uncertain. The first film I saw at the cinema with subtitles was *Chicken Run*, in 2000, a trip arranged by a local branch of the NDCS, the National Deaf Children's Society. It was incredible. Being able to sit and watch something on a huge screen and follow every bit with dialogue and sound effect captions was amazing. The second viewing was *Harry Potter and the Philosopher's Stone* the year after.

This was still early days, and I didn't often go to the cinema unless I could be confident that I would follow the story. But new subtitle technology completely changed this. I went to see films like *The Lord of the Rings* and *Harry Potter* on an equal footing with the general cinema audience. But I still couldn't pick and choose what films I wanted to see without first checking if there was a subtitled showing at Yourlocalcinema.com—and even then, I'd be lucky. At the time, it was even rare for major Hollywood blockbusters to be subtitled until a few weeks after release and at worst, a few months. I still remember going to see *Moulin Rouge* with Dan, and how he wrote down the entire plot of the movie afterwards. Luckily, he doesn't have to do that anymore, but it was frustrating and romantic in equal measure.

In the twenty-first century, it is a little—just a little!—different. Over the years, major cinema chains in the UK have stepped up their showings of subtitled cinema, with many major releases having at least one subtitled performance. But there are three major problems. One—geographical location. In London and Greater London, we have it lucky. Even if a cinema lets us down (more on that later), there is likely to be another showing somewhere else, possibly easy to get to with the tube and train network. Other places in the UK aren't that lucky. Cities do better—for example Edinburgh is good, and when I was living in York, both City Screen and the larger out of town Vue had showings, even if some were unreliable. Some people I know have had to request that cinemas show subtitled features—with varied success.

The second problem is timings. There are two types of timings that cinemas reserve for subtitled films. One is weekday evenings, perhaps 6pm, 7pm or, if you're lucky, around 8pm-9pm. But never on a Friday night. Another pattern is early on a Sunday afternoon, or early afternoon on a weekday. Perhaps they think that deaf people don't work, or don't want to see films on a Friday night, or even a Saturday night—I have never been to see a subtitled film on a Saturday night—unless it's a non-English language film.

The third, hugely disappointing and main off-putting problem for the deaf and hard of hearing cinema-going public is something that shouldn't even be an issue. Imagine travelling on the tube, train, by car, or the bus, maybe to somewhere you don't normally go, or to a couple of towns over, to see a film that you have double-checked is subtitled, maybe by phoning on text-relay, checking the cinema website, or getting a friendly hearing person to call for you. You ask the ticket-sellers if the film is subtitled. They say yes, and sell you a ticket, you buy whatever tasty snacks you want or sneak in M&Ms in your bag, and settle down to watch the adverts before the film (these are never subtitled). The film comes up, someone moves their mouth or you can hear a voice—and shock, horror!—no subtitles come up. Or they are halfway off the screen.

Your heart drops into your stomach. Perhaps another disgruntled deaf person or their hearing companion will leave the theatre to complain. Often, it has been my Mum or my husband who goes out to complain whilst I silently fume—sometimes still hopeful—in my seat. I've gone out to ask them to sort it out myself, and it is never a happy experience, because it shows how there is often a lack of communication between the employees in the cinema.

Occasionally, they restart the film with subtitles—you have every right to ask for this—which is annoying for the hearing cinemagoers, but so much more better than being sent away with an excuse, refund and free cinema tickets. It doesn't solve the problem to send people away, because the disappointment lingers. Especially if you're someone who loves cinema and films, and enjoys going out with their friends, family, and significant others (perhaps even a date). Why should you carry on going to the cinema when you're never sure if you'll actually be able to see the film?

I've discovered a number of different strategies. First, is that I have a couple of cinemas that are usually reliable. I stick to them like glue. The first one is fairly local—a twenty-minute bus ride away. The second one is in central London, a bit more awkward to get to, but not difficult. This is a good time to thank Cineworld in Enfield and the Vue Angel in Islington. There used to be an even closer one, but unfortunately it changed hands and the new cinema hasn't got its act together.

This might not be an option for those with consistently unreliable cinemas, though. In that case, I've become almost expert in writing firm but friendly emails. You should remind them that you are a paying customer, and impress upon them your absolute disappointment, whilst not blaming anyone in particular (try not to use colourful language, no matter how tempting). Keep a note of the date and time, and what happened. Follow up.

At the same time—why should deaf and hard of hearing people have to waste their energy doing something like this? The ideal is, at the very least, to be able to go to a subtitled film, and have the subtitles come up on the screen. It isn't just a random occurrence that happens once in a blue moon—it has happened to me consistently, with different cinemas, different locations, and different films. It wears away your confidence. Many people just wait for the DVDs—which is a whole other subject completely, not to mention online streaming. It's cheaper, and much more likely to be reliable.

A third option is to set up a deaf and hard of hearing cinema club with a cinema to ensure that there is a firm screening of a film each month, that will be subtitled. This is a good option for independent cinemas, and there are already a handful of subtitled cinema groups in the UK.

Even so—I feel lucky to even be able to go to a subtitled movie, no matter the potential problems. That same scent of popcorn brings back happy memories. Though I can't currently go to my local cinema where I saw my first film on the big screen—a re-release of *Snow White* with my Granny—I'm still able to go. Deaf and hard of hearing cinema patrons still have to work together to lobby cinemas and chains. Sometimes that means making cinemas aware that there is a potential larger audience that isn't being reached. There has to be a relationship built between deaf and hard of hearing patrons and cinemas—so that broken trust returns. Yes, it's frustrating and you need energy, but the rewards are magical.

Girl, Woman, Feminine, Feminist

'One is not born, but rather becomes, a woman.'

— Simone de Beauvoir, *The Second Sex.*

I was a quietly confident child. I knew my own mind and what I wanted—to read, to create, to perform, to dance, to play, to watch, to learn, to be. Freedom. My friendships at primary school began with an encounter in Reception, a girl who encouraged me to make as much mess as possible when painting in the art corner. I painted the paper on the easel. I painted the easel. I painted my hands, my arms, my face, a riot of primary colours, whilst we giggled with each other and I felt the satisfaction that comes from being a little out of control, even, perhaps, doing something bad. We were sent to the headmaster's room. The fifteen minutes I spent waiting outside the sage green door were some of the most humiliating and petrified moments I had experienced thus far in my short life. I was five, and I made a friend who would persistently ignite that desire to lose control.

I didn't know that the natural confidence I had as a child would slowly crumble the longer I stayed friends with her, and the group of girls that congregated around her. We were insular, obsessed with the label 'best friends', not understanding that it was entirely possible to just be friends with each other, and be good to each other. We ate the soul out of our friendships. There was ugly emotional violence, betrayal, instability: day to day, you could never tell whether you would arrive at school and find yourself frozen out, whispers behind cupped hands, judgemental side-eyes, the particular cruelty that young girls can do so well. I arrived one day to find implosion, the ice-wall grown tall and impenetrable, impossible to scale, and found myself reading alone in the playground.

Who knows if I would have carried on that way indefinitely, trying to sit on a bench and read, being shooed by teachers who didn't understand, or remember, the particular loneliness and confusion involved in the end of young friendships? Who couldn't, or didn't, see the cesspool of broken friendships, un-mendable betrayals trailing around the edge of the playground. Maybe they had forgotten the pain endured when you were young. After all, the first years of friendships can be formative, can teach you what it is to be a friend, what is expected of you, and the terrible games played by girls as they seek to compete with each other. We turn into our worst selves—manipulative, scheming, envious and jealous, determined to build cocoons around ourselves and the one we think is our best friend; who is, in fact, the worst of all of us.

That aloneness taught me something. Integrity. How to be true to myself, rather than following the crowd. It also taught me something else—that there are always people who will take notice, understand what you are going through, and extend the hand of honest friendship, without expectations. What a revelation it was to be friends with someone who didn't call me 'best friend', who was, instead, a loyal, caring, and empathetic companion. She was close friends with another girl, but I had learnt my lesson and tried hard not to tread on anyone's toes. A number of times that old fear and envy returned, as the old group of girls tried playing games, tried to lure this new friend away, but she didn't like playing games. I didn't either, any longer.

What happens when you opt out of game playing in friendship? You learn to appreciate what you get, rather than heaping expectations on anyone. It took me years to realise that what I craved wasn't best friends, but depth. A handful of good friends. People I could talk to, without having to hide myself. When people mistake depth for clinginess, for exclusivity, they panic. More betrayals and hurts awaited me in the future, but at that moment, I was happy, and content, and understood that I had made a friend who would never treat me badly. It restored my trust in other people. My suspicions were confirmed when I witnessed the kind of playground girl on girl gang bullying that ended in a cataclysmic event: a kick that sounded like a pistol shot, and a girl doubled over in pain. We were only ten, maybe eleven by that point. It knocked the breath out of me, seeing the emotional cruelty made manifest.

Cat's Eye by Margaret Atwood is an extreme example of how the cruelty of girlhood friendships and bullying can get out of control and can lead to later problems finding and maintaining friendships as women. An artist, back in the city of Toronto for a retrospective of her art, reminisces about her childhood, and in particular the friendships she made with a group of girls. Elaine is naive in many respects, and unknowing about conventional expectations of femininity (and the hidden rules) because of her unconventional upbringing travelling with her parents—her father is an entomologist and her mother is a free-thinking independent woman. Eventually, Elaine's naivety leads to the girls, and a newcomer, Cordelia, exploiting her lack of knowledge in order to bully her. Becoming caught up in cruel games of friendship and bullying can be common with girls of primary school age and beyond—the first indoctrination into the pressures of what it means to be female in this society—in competition with each other, learning unhealthy behaviours. The boys in the playground were active, playing football or card games, or chasing girls in games of 'tag'. Are girls socialised early to become objects, to play psychological games, and to put their energy into intrigues rather than anything creative and fun?

Secondary school was more confusion and survival. I had good friends, and people in my year who were friendly, but my awkwardness and sometimes debilitating shyness didn't allow me to reach out into a wider world of possible friendships. I stayed within the deaf circle of friends I made through the support unit, though there were a small number of hearing friends in the first two years that I spent time with. The school, after my small primary school experience, was overwhelming. Hundreds of teenagers attended this school. It was a good school at the time, and in hindsight there were many wonderful and rewarding moments. I was lucky enough to learn Sociology, to have a series of encouraging English teachers, and to do Art as a GCSE.

In the third year (year 9), a nervousness and anxiety overcame me, to the point that I was afraid of everything. I was afraid of my peers. Inside I was struggling, afraid of being judged by everyone, and feeling like an outsider. My only escape was books, and the handful of friends I had, along with my involvement in performing at Chickenshed Theatre. I was split down the middle, two different people, full of fear and embarrassment on one hand, on the other, mostly away from the place, quietly confident, sometimes even bolshy, with a zany sense of humour. I frustrated myself. I felt resentful towards people who tried to force me to be someone I wasn't. Outside I may have appeared standoffish and quiet, a little cold, whilst inside I was a technicolour mess, trying to control my reactions and anxiety.

Maybe it was this internal struggle, or some misplaced envy, that made it easier for a deaf girl in my class to start bullying me. To start with, it just felt annoying, even embarrassing, as she kicked me under the table in class, and followed me around, insinuating herself on my friends, small little annoying encroachments on my personal space. She would send barbed comments my way, commenting on my body. Eventually, these annoyances sunk in, creating even more of an oppressive atmosphere. I confided, eventually, to my Mum, and we spoke to someone in the HIU, who arranged a cringeworthy one-to-one meeting between this girl and me. I felt as though she was laughing at me, as though she had somehow won her game, despite being foiled. At least the overt bullying stopped, though the damage to my confidence took some years to heal. I came to understand that she had her own issues to deal with, and though that doesn't excuse her behaviour, I tried to find a way to forgive her.

My sister attended the same school in the last few years I was there. This coincided with my final year of GCSEs and my first year of A Levels, which was a difficult time for my friendships. The girls I considered close friends decided to cut ties with me—I couldn't describe it any other way because of the literal way they told me they didn't want to spend as much time with me. I saw them less and less, and relied more on friends outside school. My closest friend became more distant because she was preparing to leave for university (she was a year older). Until finally, I found myself dealing with that familiar loneliness from the playground. I spent time with my sister at lunchtimes, and we became closer. I doubt I would have managed the sting of feeling alone without her and her friends, who I am still so thankful for. It was my life outside of school where I fully came alive—performing with Chickenshed Theatre, and a few close friends made through those productions.

Opting into femininity started early. The lie of a certain type of sanitised, able-bodied, imperfection-free beauty: that women and girls need to look good, that their worth is based on their appearance. It wasn't my Mum I learnt this from, though sometimes she wasn't immune to it. It was other girls, and magazines, and the first few role models from popular culture. It was the nineties, so I was lucky that this was an era that gave us the *Spice Girls*, *All Saints*, *TLC*, and Gwen Stefani of *No Doubt*. Yes, they all wore makeup and they were arguably also 'types' in that way the music industry deems palatable, but they didn't fit the typical mould of pop star. The *Spice Girls* were bold, and loud, giving us a bright, though easy to digest, version of empowerment. *All Saints* were interesting, style-wise—baggy 'combat' trousers, little vest tops, beanie hats, nose piercings. Along with Gwen Stefani, the lead singer of *No Doubt*, they represented a kind of looser, freer style, not about impressing boys, but about impressing ourselves.

The two magazines that changed the way I saw the world and typified the era I grew up in, were J17 and a short-lived but empowering magazine called Jump. This was before I started reading magazines for women (Cosmo, Marie Claire, etc). They were fun, joyful, had useful advice, and in the case of Jump, looked at more serious topics around self-esteem and body acceptance. This was the earliest inkling I had of what it meant to accept myself. At that point I didn't: I had been indoctrinated into comparing myself with other girls, hated my body, didn't like what I saw in the mirror, and equated my self-worth with what I looked like.

Why did I feel this way? I saw the girls around me doing the same. They had days when they said they felt fat, code for 'ugly'. Imagine, as someone who was the chubbiest girl in our friendship group, hearing that my body was code for 'ugly'. They had days when they spoke about what they were eating, in detail, and that they needed to go on a diet. Even the adult women around me were constantly dieting. Nobody was happy with the way they looked. I considered all of them beautiful. I wish I had told them more often that they looked wonderful, that they inspired me, and that I appreciated them. That they could rock platform Buffalo shoes and flares better than the *Spice Girls*. That their smiles lit up the whole room. That it was the best thing ever when we laughed breathlessly, tears in our eyes, and forgot, just for a little while, about the way we looked, or didn't look.

The terrible thing is, this behaviour is widespread. Someone will say 'I look terrible today'. Someone else will reply, 'no, you don't, don't be silly! I look even worse! Look at my terrible spots and my double chin!' We have made insulting ourselves into an Olympic sport. We don't treat ourselves with kindness. We don't look into the mirror and think about how lovely we look, how our faces are us, and we deserve all the love we send our way. We look how we look, and it's only the surface. It's only skin and bones, hair and flesh. Yes, it can be beautiful, but what is more important? The way we look, or what we do and how we behave, who we are, what we create, and what we share? Appearance is only important if you want to be a model, or, arguably, act in Hollywood—though even then, there are many unconventional actresses, lauded for their acting skills.

My own definition of beauty, after I stopped reading women's magazines, expanded. I see beauty everywhere. I've stopped comparing myself to other women. Conventional magazines are ground zero of bad self-esteem in women, and even, increasingly, for men—they have such contradictory messages contained within. There are the gossip pages, where other women's bodies are dissected, cellulite mocked, weight loss or weight gain scrutinised, plastic surgery speculated upon. Then there are the features that talk about mental health, the latest diet, how to improve self-esteem, and how to look good for a man or 'for yourself'. Pages of fashion that you can't afford and beauty products that could bankrupt you. As a teen, I bought a lot. Teens nowadays often buy a lot too. We buy into the idea that beauty can be bought, that it should be bought, that we need to improve ourselves through products that say they will solve all our problems. The beauty industry created cellulite in order to sell us products that will 'cure' it—it's just normal female skin.

And then there's the narrowing of representations of different body types, both men and women. There's a certain slim margin of acceptable body types, never mind that in real life, you see all kinds of bodies, everywhere. There's this mythical ideal that gets fed to us, from the time we become aware of our own body, to the time we are fully grown. I am, and have always been, a large body type. Either curvy or fat (in a reclaimed sense of the word), I have struggled with the fact that my body wasn't represented in any of the media I consumed as a child or as a teen, and as a young adult. Larger bodies are seen as wrong, bad, unhealthy, unattractive, something to laugh at, in need of changing, a temporary shell. Dehumanised. In fact, we all dehumanise bodies, all types of them. We see them as somehow separate from ourselves, a shell rather than as a whole, cohesive, interesting aspect of who we are. Being deaf too, has been a challenge on the route towards body acceptance. Deaf people in popular culture were figures of fun, or people to be pitied, or alien and sexual (as in the beginning of *Children of a Lesser God*).

It is no wonder that it's so hard to heal ourselves. We are spoon fed ideas and unhealthy ideals from the world around us. From the people around us. And the only way to feel better is to take a stark look at what it is that is having such an adverse effect on the way you see yourself. For me, as I've mentioned, one of them was women's magazines. So, I stopped reading them. I couldn't find a magazine like Jump that bridged the gap between teenagehood and womanhood. I read books that helped me understand the difference between an artificial construct of beauty and what is personal to me. What did I—do I—love or like about myself? How could I let go of comparing myself to other women? How could I show the wonderful women in my life that they are beautiful, and amazing? How could I use makeup, 'beauty' products, and clothing, to make myself feel good rather than buying in to the idea that I'm not enough?

I refused to wear dresses for some time after childhood. The first time I wore a dress again was in my early twenties. I was a teenager in the nineties and early noughties, a time of girl power, baggy utility trousers, grunge, and small strappy vests. I kept this style even at university, choosing to wear my large, baggy black skate trousers with little t-shirts, colourful and pretty vests, and cardigans. I was, to all intents and purposes, someone who thought dresses were impractical and uncomfortable. One summer, though, I started wearing dresses over jeans and cropped trousers. I chose jewel colours to wear: rich purples, deep teals, royal and bright blues. Clothes became an expression of my internal life, an expression of my love for pattern and colour. Style was joy and confidence.

This colour represented something of a metamorphosis. At university, I found it difficult to make friends, though I did try. In the second year, I moved into a house with two other women. By the third year, one of the women had left, whilst the other became prickly, excluding me from evenings out, though she had been friendly and warm the year before. I cared less about this than I had with past friendships. I felt that I had close friends and family who appreciated me, and though her behaviour stung, it was the last year and I was determined to do well. I enjoyed my independence, and would regularly go into York's town centre by myself for a coffee and to read a book, to visit bookshops, and browse DVDs. Occasionally, I went to subtitled showings of films by myself too, and enjoyed the independent solitude. The difference was that it was my time to do something for myself, to take care of myself—I rarely felt lonely, and when I did, it was usually homesickness, and missing friends or Dan.

This was in stark contrast to my experience doing my Master's degree two years later in York again. I was more self-assured, independent, and studying in the small but close-knit interdisciplinary Women's Studies department. There was something about being in an environment that celebrated and encouraged the achievements of women—all the women in my year became firm friends. I got to know two of them well, through campaigning activities on campus, shared interests, and joining the Student Union Women's Committee. We often met in pubs, drank pints of cider, and spoke for hours, making up a new game of Pictionary, Feminist Pictionary, and ordering chips when we got hungry. If there was ever a proper definition of the feminist ideal of 'sisterhood', this was it. We all helped each other, giving encouragement, support, and working together. I was an active member of the feminist community, attending Reclaim the Night marches in London, blogging furiously about feminism, and examining my own beliefs and ideals. It was a good year, a time of social confidence and learning more about myself and the world around me, something that was missing during my Bachelor's degree.

It was doing my Master's degree that led me towards writing again. My dissertation was a cathartic journey—social research into deaf women's lives and autobiographies, attempting to find where their identities as woman and deaf intersected, how these aspects of themselves interacted. By the end of it all, I wanted to carry on—to keep writing, to keep digging into my experiences and ideas. In a roundabout way, then, feminism has been my way into writing. Perhaps this isn't surprising, considering the sources that inspired me during my research—notably Hélène Cixous's 'Laugh of the Medusa'—her wonderful, powerful entreaty for women:

'Write! Writing is for you, you are for you; your body is yours, take it. I know why you haven't written. (And why I didn't write before the age of twenty-seven.) Because writing is at once too high, too great for you, it's reserved for the great-that is for "great men"; and it's "silly."'

— Hélène Cixous, *The Laugh of the Medusa*.

Emmanuelle Laborit's *The Cry of the Gull* and her essay on language and words also inspired me to take up my own stories. What is striking about both *The Cry of the Gull*, Laborit's autobiography, and '*The Laugh of the Medusa*' is that they focus on women's becoming and expression through language, the body, and words. For me, it was a clarion call, a waking up and realisation that I wanted, more than anything, to write and live a life of purpose. The expectations girls and women have to be a certain way, to be nice, and polite, pretty, and hide away their deepest potential, their secret longings, does the world a disservice. Imagine—all the ideas, inventions, songs, books, solutions, possibilities—locked up within half of the human race. To bring that out of ourselves, we have to spend less time worrying about what we look like, and more time being human, imperfect.

At the same time, the contradiction is of course, that there is nothing wrong with using clothes, make-up, scent, and style to express ourselves. I view it as one particular aspect of self-expression: it's not my best or my most important way of expressing myself and feeling good, but it's one of them. The problem is that we don't participate in beauty practices in a vacuum, and everything we do is within a culture that doesn't fully respect women as autonomous, whole, and independent human beings. Sexism and misogyny continue to be real, painful, facts of our existence on earth. Until we change—until the culture changes, and our legal and social systems change—we will still have girls and women who won't reach their full potential. So yes, by all means, we can have fun with self-expression, but we still live in a culture that preys on self-esteem and looks at the female body (and, increasingly, the male body) as a problem to be solved. A sense of liberation comes, for both men and women, not to mention trans, non-binary, and neutral gendered people, when we let go of gender stereotypes, when we can pick and choose how we are seen, and are accepted for that. This is a privilege that only some of us have. We're not out of the woods yet, because there are movements that have been fighting for centuries to be seen as human, as equal, and as whole.

Maybe I'm quieter about feminism these days because I'm torn between anger and a feeling of powerlessness. I've accepted that nobody can change society and culture on their own—you need a movement, and a community with you. You often have to choose the niche you want to work on. I support different causes and issues how and when I can, but yet, I know it's not enough. What we need is a sea-change in culture and attitudes, an awakening and educating so that societies change and bring the potential out of everyone. This is why the work of feminism is demanding and difficult, because it's both about becoming more aware of intersections and different voices, and about working with others for a brighter future. Maybe the 'Time's Up' and 'Me Too' campaigns are some of the best examples of this. It's a challenge to the dominant, patriarchal systems we live within. First of all, though, it begins with you—with each of us—seeing through a lens that exposes what lies beneath.

Modern Tragedy

On the morning of 15th July 2016, I awoke to the news that the previous night there had been another attack in Nice, France. A lorry had ploughed into people celebrating Bastille Day, on the Promenade des Anglais, killing around eighty people, and injuring countless others as they tried to escape the carnage.

My heart is tired, and I know that many of us are also feeling that heaviness of a tired, weary, soul, seeing the world hurting, each day another place with people dead. Is it globalisation that makes us feel closer to events that have happened elsewhere? I only know that there is a sense of helplessness, that each time something happens, I run out of words. We all know. We all know this feeling. There is only so many times we can say, in a Facebook status or a series of tweets, how sad we are. Twenty-four-hour news, skimming over the same comments and headlines, empty speculation, and a climate of anxiety, do none of us any good.

I still remember the feeling of impending, horrified doom when I came home one afternoon after school, to see the twin towers burning and collapsing. Everything since then has been chaotic, at least to my eyes. War has always been happening somewhere, always far away. Terror attacks have become more commonplace, part of the texture of life in the twenty-first century. Of course, we can trace how they began, of course we can see how the pattern emerged if we care to look deeper. Most of us don't look too closely because we are content to read headlines and move on to the next thing the next day. It is worth trying to understand the situation in more detail because that way, we can see the machinations of global governments, wars over oil and borders, a tale of fundamentalist warmongers and dangerous idealists—Christian, Islamic and otherwise—that complicates the shallow headlines we see day in and day out. People declaring war in the name of a religion doesn't mean that the religion is inherently bad. Particularly not when the vast majority of participants in a religion are peaceful, law-abiding citizens.

Patriotism is meaningless to me. I'm not someone who glorifies the monarchy or feels that we should be proud of our country. We have a history of colonialism and slavery. We also have a tradition of immigrant communities—when much of our culture and cuisine comes from cultures other than our own. For example, fish and chips are said to come from a Jewish immigrant, Joseph Malin, who set up shop in London, and tea was imported from China and India. Essentially, we are a country of immigrant cultures. I feel far more part of a global community than part of a country, where the values of our government have shifted and warped, and where I no longer feel as if my vote counts for much. I still vote—women and men fought hard for the right to vote. My disillusionment with government and the establishment mean that I am under no illusions that, with our current first past the post system, voting for anything I believe in is pointless. I can only vote for the Labour party or the Conservative party. I would much rather vote for the Greens, or for a progressive party that doesn't even exist. My values and the policies I most care about seem to land somewhere between the far left and the middle, down where the human rights activists congregate.

So where do you look when you need to make sense of the world, and need to find a measure of healing? Not to people who want to create further divisions, who want to go to war, who are dismantling what we can be proud of in this country—the NHS and our welfare system. No, we have to look to each other. It's the only way to deal with the immensity of what is happening in the world. We can also look within and try to find some peace. For me, despite my sense of wordlessness at the tragedy surrounding us, I try to write. I found it difficult to write the day after the Nice attack, in the middle of writing this book. Maybe in the midst of tragedy we can find some resilience, even hope.

The problem is that we are at war. The world is at war. War, such an ugly, short word. It is drawn out, not short and sharp. Humans are killing each other. Daesh wants us all to be afraid. This is what terrorism is—it wants us to stay in, stop living, become anxious and fearful. It wants to spread intolerance and create divisions, for us to be at each other's throats. It is about destroying unity and sowing suspicion. By claiming ownership of Islam, it wants to pin its brand of terror onto peaceful, non-violent citizens. Terrorists are not the people who go about their daily lives, but intelligent, resourceful recruits. They know how media works, how the internet works – and just how they can use that to make us feel afraid, even afraid of each other.

The biggest fight for us is to be unafraid. To learn to find peace within ourselves and to learn to care for each other. Understand that events like this—in Nice, in Baghdad, in Paris, in Istanbul, Manchester, Syria—are painful and defy understanding, and we are going to be sad, devastated, angry—but we have each other. In the midst of everything, we can make our own place of stillness and acceptance. We can support the causes that matter to us, we can welcome people and make them feel accepted. We can walk in solidarity with people who are disaffected, disillusioned, and broken-hearted. Instead of allowing our hearts to become hard, we can allow them to expand, and mend them for each other. Nourish your soul, and be better, and good to each other.

Though today my heart is tired, I am still trying not to allow myself to give up. I am still trying not to be afraid and anxious. I'm accepting that we have no control over what other people choose to do, but we do have control over how we react, and who we choose to be. Even in the midst of uncertainty, I can choose to let go of my fears, accept what is, grieve the loss of life, and hope for a better tomorrow.

Deaf Identities

Deaf identity is something both ever-evolving and traditionally determined by history, culture, education, language and community. Historically, deaf people have been defined by two major 'identities'—oral and signing—mainly because type of education and upbringing separated deaf people into these two categories. For the most part, there are two types of education available for deaf people: mainstream education or education in a deaf school.

Mainstream education involves either placing a deaf child in a school with an HIU (hearing impaired unit) or PDS (provision for deaf students), or the council providing support workers (sign language interpreters or notetakers for example). There are few deaf schools left in the UK—just over 20—so most deaf children attend mainstream schools, often without enough support to cover all their lessons if they receive support at all. Most of the time, parents have to work hard to make sure councils give their children the support they need in order to pursue an education equal to that of their hearing peers.

My 'deaf identity' probably looks straightforward to most. I grew up in a hearing family, went to a mainstream primary without an HIU, occasionally supported by an in-class teacher of the deaf. I followed this by going to a large London secondary with an HIU, mixed with mainstream peers, and thrived academically—but experienced the mainstream effect of friendship problems, anxiety, and some loneliness.

To start with, I was given the label 'hearing-impaired', by audiologists and teachers. This was mid-to-late eighties, and time has moved on. I moved on. I stopped referring to myself as hearing-impaired when I was a teenager and understood that I didn't feel comfortable with that label any longer. Impairment suggests a reliance on physical features, as if there is something profoundly wrong with you. Some of the deaf teenagers around me still carried on using that term, and whilst I felt it was their own choice, I still felt as if it was a label imposed upon us. What happens when you feel you've stepped into another identity? I know that when people see the word 'deaf', this also comes with assumptions and ideas about what that looks like. It covers a whole spectrum of deafness, from partially deaf, to fully deaf. For me, the word 'deaf' is less a label, than an acceptance of part of my self—my body, my identity, my experiences.

Beyond the physical, medical definitions of my deaf identity, it has been a rollercoaster. At times, I've been confused, felt a need for belonging—to what, I'm never sure. I used to wonder if it was belonging to community I needed, in this case, the deaf community. Or if I wanted to belong more to the hearing world. Why has it been so important to me, to discover completeness, having a place to belong? The truth is, most humans, though they might have their own communities, family units, relationships, identity, only truly belong to themselves. It's imperative that we belong to ourselves because we are complete human beings.

Instead of finding that lonely, I find it comforting to know that I can look after myself, and that I can then connect with other human beings through love, respect, and shared interests. Identity is an ever-shifting, ever-changing sense of self. We like patterns, as humans. We like to neatly put people, and ourselves, into categories and labels, making it so that sometimes, we are held back, heavy with expectations and culture. Belonging is a thorny topic, because we long for human connection, and to be alone in our individuality can be painful, but the alternative is conformity and the possibility of never truly living, being awake, never questioning what makes us uncomfortable.

With a deaf sister, I didn't feel like my deafness itself was a problem, but that there were many access and communication barriers within society, education, and services. Since my deafness became worse after I had acquired language (as did my sister's), I was already an English speaker, writer—and obviously, a voracious reader, encouraged by our parents. British sign language (BSL), the fingerspelling alphabet, and the idea of a deaf community came a little later.

Socialising with other deaf children and adult role models through our local NDCS (National Deaf Children's Society), I was lucky enough that my sense of identity as a deaf person didn't include feelings of isolation or a sense of 'lack'. I could still do the what I loved to do, and I was encouraged to explore what interested me and that I was good at as a child. Looking back, I realise how important this is when you're a deaf child. Role models, access to language—either BSL or speech or both, whichever is the easiest for the child to pick up (because they are both legitimate, complex languages), positive reinforcement and encouragement, and ways for a child to express themselves—this means that as we grow up, deaf people have a positive understanding of their own identity. They help you get through the challenges, all the barriers to push through, the inevitably difficult moments.

This is where the messiness creeps in. I dislike calling myself 'oral', because though it's my most used means of communication, it doesn't mean that this is how I see myself. Maybe to some deaf people I am 'oral' because it's the way I've been brought up. I respect BSL as a language with its own grammar structure, linguistics, and history, and how it has changed over time. I picked up some of it here and there through performing on stage signing songs at Chickenshed, through informal lessons, and through using it with deaf friends when I was younger. It has always been there. On the periphery. It's not my prime method of communication, because somehow, I feel a little awkward signing. It depends who I'm with, and how comfortable I feel. I know, deep down, that I have a good grasp of vocabulary, that my receptive skills ('reading' sign language) are fair, and that when comfortable, I can get into a flow. And, around seven years ago, I jumped at the chance to learn level 2 formally with my sister, after learning level 1 as part of my AS Levels twelve years ago.

Then there's how I feel about speaking too. As I mentioned in an earlier essay, '*Indolence: The Pleasure of Doing Nothing*', my voice is quiet—mostly because this is just the way my voice is. At school, I developed a complex about it, and as a result, worry about whether or not I'm loud enough in hearing company. In deaf company, it tends not to matter as much, because we use a mix of communication methods—from lipreading, to BSL and SSE (sign supported English)—whatever works. My preference is as open and adaptable as possible. I may not always feel comfortable in my own BSL proficiency, but I still consider it part of my communication repertoire. The truth is, everyone has their own 'signing voice'— their own way of signing, and when part of informal company, that's fine. Maybe as we get older, we grow into feeling more comfortable with who we are, the way we speak, and the way we express ourselves. It matters less what people think of us, so long as we are comfortable with ourselves.

Most people I know in the UK deaf community are lovely, and wouldn't dream of excluding people, or imposing their own views, or demanding that you change your identity to fit in. But I have experienced exclusion and community judgement, as well as in-fighting. I have also come into contact with people who can't see (or don't care about) the damage they do to those around them, and leave people dealing with the aftermath. People who are convinced that their way is the best way. As a result, it has been difficult to rebuild my understanding of my personal deaf identity. I've always felt that I can adapt, but part of me recoils from being too involved in deaf politics or building my whole identity around deaf culture. I'm wary of the binary that we put ourselves in. Because our thinking is that there are only two types of deaf people—those who can sign, and those who are 'oral', we end up excluding and polarising each other. So many people are now bilingual—can both sign, and speak, or write. Just because you might not be part of the deaf community, doesn't also mean you don't understand what it's like, to be a sign-language user in a world of sound and an audio-centric society.

I feel that within my generation, ages 20-30-something, there is much more understanding of how it feels to be in the middle of something, to be a part of a deaf world, and a hearing world, yet not completely belong to either. Most of my close friends are deaf, though my parents, extended family, and husband are hearing. The people within my age group seem to have fluidity, yet also individuality, within their deaf identities. I find myself considering what it all means to be in the middle, neither here nor there. But humans are contradictions, and we hold so many contradictory traits, behaviours, and beliefs anyway. We can't be all one thing, we are things by degrees.

Communication access is the biggest, most important thing, regardless of anything else. This includes subtitling and captioning, speech to text, technology that works (there are many current problems with speech recognition apps), lipspeakers, BSL interpreters. I do understand, though, that the fight for global sign languages to be recognised is hugely important, because this should lead to better access to interpreters and better training. It should lead to better understanding and deaf awareness. Or, that is the hope. Deaf awareness is more complicated than just—she's deaf, she signs—or he's deaf, he lipreads. And deafness can have a major psychological and social impact because it's all about how we communicate with each other, being as inclusive as possible, learning how to adapt to the company you're in. For some, that's difficult, but it reaps so many rewards, and can improve your communication across the board.

I'm comfortable with the label 'deaf', though it also invites questions, and curiosity. People want to know—'how much can you hear?' or 'do you know sign-language?' And on the surface, I understand. We want to know about what it's like to not have one of our senses at 'full' capacity, whatever that might mean. I would rather that people didn't ask me this because it puts the spotlight on what I can't do, immediately focusing on the physical reality as opposed to the individual standing in front of you. To learn to appreciate someone as a person, as someone who has their own thing going on, rather than focusing on ability, is a much more humanising and respectful thing to do. It's important to ask people what their communication preferences are, but beyond this, getting to know someone before you ask about how much they can hear is best. I feel that most people want to be known for what they can do, what they're interested in, and who they are, rather than for anything else.

Still, this isn't to ignore the real and sometimes awkward realities of being a deaf person. It can be socially isolating, especially when you live in the 'hearing world' and your family and friends, workmates, and society at large is hearing. Informing others of your communication needs can become second nature—don't talk too fast, or too slow (no miming, please!), don't cover your mouth, don't shout, avoid standing in front of light and becoming a dark looming shadowed thing, and allow pauses in conversation so that someone can keep up and formulate an answer. On most occasions, it's a struggle, because despite people's best intentions, hearing conversation features a lot of fast banter, covering of mouths with hands, chewing and talking at the same time, having to look down to eat your food and looking up to find something completely different being discussed. You become reliant, despite it all, on a few well-meaning individuals to recap the conversation for you. Lip-reading becomes tiring and downright exhausting after a while. You're using your eyes as a language processing tool, and it needs a lot of guesswork, filling in the gaps, and time to understand what you're seeing. So yes, being deaf is also hard work, and the struggles are there.

My identity as a deaf person, then, is also defined by this—by this using my eyes far more than the average hearing person. I think in images, much of the time, and I use visual tools like Pinterest in ways that express moods, ideas, and thought. My fiction writing also tends to be visually oriented. Art and illustration, design, and typography—in short, things that are visually interesting and beautiful are important to me. I feel that though not all deaf people are interested so much in the visual, it is still a part of our inner landscape, whether or not that is something we are conscious of. My eyes, I feel, are my most important way of accessing the world.

My deafness is a constantly changing aspect of my identity. My comfort with it changes over time. Sometimes, faced with social complications, with feeling disheartened with how much I can't access in hearing society, I want to give up and retreat. Other times, I feel as though it gives me a different, even interesting, perspective on the world, and I'm grateful for the chance to write about it. I've met many interesting people throughout my life who I wouldn't have met otherwise. It has had different effects on the people I've met too—who haven't met a deaf person before—and who have had their world-view broadened. I try to be gracious and understanding when people ask me questions about being a deaf person, because maybe the encounter will make them more aware of how to communicate with another deaf person. Being curious, after all, is a human trait that means we can empathise and learn to understand other people.

Writing through the contradictions, I'm reminded that

sometimes, you don't have to 'be' anything. It is only through our contact with others that we feel we have to quantify who and what we are. The more I go through life, the more I understand that sometimes, it doesn't matter. Identity isn't necessarily about the components, but about the whole. Humans are messy and complicated, bits of us might be broken or confusing, and some of us might still be trying to work out who we are. There are always more questions than answers.

How To Be A Geek

It was John Green, the author of *The Fault in Our Stars* and *Paper Towns*, who said in an interview that being a geek (or a nerd) is literally just being unabashedly enthusiastic about something. John Green knows what he is talking about—he set up a channel on YouTube with his brother Hank Green, in which they have explained everything from science phenomena to the unemployment rate. They also have an army of followers calling themselves 'Nerdfighters'.

'Nerdfighteria' originally came about through a joke when John misread the name of a video game as Nerd Fighters, and finding it funny, in a vlog he said: "Here's my question about *Nerdfighters*: is *Nerdfighters* a game about people who fight against nerds, or is it a game about nerds who fight against other people? I've come to believe that *Nerdfighters* is a game about nerds who fight, nerds who tackle the scourge of popular people. And I've been thinking to myself... this would be a great video game."

His community is a port in the storm of feeling like an outsider within society, and doing good, such as getting involved in charity initiatives, creating, and using logic to solve problems in the world. His novels are popular often because the characters are offbeat, teenagers who don't feel that they clearly 'fit in' for whatever reason. For example, *The Fault in Our Stars* is about two teens with cancer who fall in love and navigate their lives living on the periphery of culture—both characters are unconventional protagonists. The Green brothers set up a foundation, 'The Foundation to Decrease World Suck', a non-profit devoted to raising money for charitable organisations, connected to their 'Nerdfighteria' community and YouTube channel.

Unlike the popular definition of being a nerd or geek meaning you are an unproductive or negative member of society, obsessed with a particular cultural niche, 'Nerdfighteria' is all about using your nerdiness as a way to make society better. My own early forays into science fiction, fantasy, supernatural horror, and being a book geek led me towards activism. In many ways, it was inevitable— being a woman, being deaf, and feeling like an outsider in a largely white male geek community, meant becoming more aware of cultural bias, stereotypes and lack of representation. Being a fan of *Star Wars*, and being a woman, for example, elicits two responses— either 'awesome', or 'prove to us how much of a fan you are'. Even the former answer comes with reservations—the idea that it is unusual for a woman to enjoy science fiction or space operas. Especially given the original trilogy's main character is Luke Skywalker, and not Leia Organa. Leia has her own appeal as a role model—she has become General Organa, the leader of the resistance, and she was a wise-cracking and strong-minded character in the original three films.

Being a geek has traditionally come with a host of negative perceptions, viewed as a laughing stock or as 'uncool'. When I was at school, people identified as geeks were generally intelligent, interested in science, computers, and comic books. With the internet came an expansion of the idea of 'geek'—suddenly it became more acceptable to know about computers, technology, and websites. The community culture that sprung up with the net enabled like-minded people to form groups around their interests, such as the aforementioned comic books. The growth of tech industries, the importance of coding, and Silicon Valley companies

217

mean that it is no longer 'niche' to have a career formerly thought of as geeky. People working in these industries are celebrated.

With social media, geekhood has never been more acceptable. People are no longer afraid of proclaiming their deep love of *Star Wars* or Marvel's *Avengers*. On Instagram, literary book lovers, lit-geeks, share beautiful photos of their books and bookcases, giving mini-reviews and sharing their love of everything bookish. Science fiction fans review sci-fi movies and games, and of course the gaming community has millions of people on Twitter. Geeks care less about how people see them, and more about how much they love their thing, or things. In that way, I think that being a geek is one of the best things it is possible to be—what better way to live than to celebrate other people's creations and be inspired to create your own? People who write read voraciously. People who code might spend hours playing games. People who love Marvel or DC (or both!) are inspired to cosplay and go to conventions.

I used to think a lot about being 'cool' and what that meant. Especially when I was a teenager, awkward and self-tortured and worried about what other people thought. The most popular people in my year were extroverted and had an aura of 'cool', whatever you might define that as. Perhaps the concept of what is 'cool' is different all over the world. I didn't consider myself 'cool', or at least I didn't feel I came across that way to other people.

In some ways, coolness seemed to be about whoever could shine the brightest, who paid attention to how they looked to others in terms of behaviour, mannerisms, and who they hung out with. It also seemed to be about not expressing too much interest in pursuits beyond popular music, fashion, and consumerism. In those respects, I felt decidedly uncool, even though the people I was friends with were probably some of the 'coolest' people I knew—they loved what they loved, and were always ahead of the trends. Over time, as I became a little more confident, I lost the desire to be 'cool'; it might have been a strain to always be in the limelight, maintaining that kind of control over your identity.

Of course, too, being a girl as a teenager comes with all kinds of pressures. When you're also highly sensitive and prone to embarrassment, and even shame, school is a minefield of accidents waiting to happen. Being famously clumsy, I had a number of memorable embarrassing moments—such as tripping over down the stairs taking a boy in my class with me, or that time when I had to run a bleep test with the wrong kind of leggings in my PE kit (imagine running from wall to wall hoisting up cut off tights that didn't quite fit properly). I was far away from the idea of 'cool' portrayed in high school movies, and now I feel as if that was valuable. It taught me to be more resilient, and to value what mattered most—friendship, family, what I genuinely loved doing, watching, and reading, and thinking for myself. The embarrassing moments I remember with a shudder, but also with fond kindness— I didn't allow them to stop me from facing each day at school.

I started thinking of myself as a geek, albeit a closeted geek, when I began to own how much I loved reading, sci-fi and fantasy, and other equally so-called 'uncool' things. I'm not sure if they are considered as geeky as they used to be, but I don't exaggerate when I say I truly love *Star Wars*, and the theme music gives me a little thrill of excitement every time I hear it. Maybe what we love is somehow fixed by the era we grew up in—in my case the mid-late 80s, 90s, and early 00s—but I still find all kinds of new culture and ideas to geek about and be obsessed with.

In my early twenties, I read whatever I could get my hands on about Marilyn Monroe and Audrey Hepburn, and watched all their films. I still enjoy their films but maybe not as much as I did. This pattern repeats itself often—I find something I'm excited about, and won't stop until I've immersed myself completely in it. Some interests stay longer than others—an example is the Studio Ghibli films (*My Neighbour Totoro*, *Howl's Moving Castle*), which myself and my husband still watch and love. I also went through a phase of watching Asian action movies, French films, and South American and Mexican films—particularly films by Pedro Almodovar, Alejandro Gonzalez Inarritu, and Guillermo del Toro, director of *The Shape of Water* and *Pan's Labyrinth*. Exploring different topics and genres gives me inspiration for my own work and keeps my curiosity alive.

Being a woman and a geek comes with its own challenges. Quite apart from the 'surprise' when I talk about science fiction and fantasy, women have struggled in online communities and on social media with sharing their opinions and driving discussion around representation and sexism. One such example is when Anita Sarkeesian's *Tropes vs. Women in Video Games* educational video series about the questionable depiction of women in videogames raised money on Kickstarter and made her a target of a hate campaign on the Internet. Another example is when Zoe Quinn, a game creator, became the victim of a campaign of hate and abuse when a spurned ex-boyfriend posted a forum post about her. The resulting abuse organised itself under the hashtag 'Gamergate'. Internet abuse and trolling is almost guaranteed when you are a visible woman within a community that has largely thought of itself as white and male. So why do geeky women bother to keep fighting?

Geek culture has been largely controlled by and dominated by men who want to indulge in nostalgia. Women, often because we want to change the status-quo—to have more equal representation, to imagine a better future, to create media that isn't dominated by white male characters—are pushed against because of fear. If you think about how the new incarnations of *Ghostbusters* (with Melissa McCarthy, Kristen Wiig, Kate McKinnon and Leslie Jones) and *Star Wars* (with Daisy Ridley, John Boyega, and Oscar Isaac) have female characters at the helm, and the resulting outcry from many male fans online, you can see how the pattern manifests. It doesn't matter that women make up roughly 50 per cent of the world's population, if not a little less according to the latest statistics. If women, LGBTQA people, and people of colour and non-Western cultures want better for the world, and the stories we create involve trying to have a more balanced ratio of characters, then inevitably people trying to uphold the status-quo want to carry on as they are, because they benefit the most from the power imbalance.

Falling in love with culture and life is really what geekhood is about. Allowing yourself to be excited and enthusiastic about something. Maybe other people won't be as excited as you, but you are bound to find a community or group of people out there who are. I don't believe there should be qualifiers about 'how much' of a fan you are—I feel like the more the merrier when it comes to expressing our abiding love for something. And if you are part of the ongoing creating of media and culture that plugs the gaps and imagines a better future, then don't give up. Persistence is key. We are only on this planet for a limited time, and should be able to feel free to create or be involved in and enjoy culture, art, science, astronomy, films, books, and whatever else there is to appreciate about this planet of ours. Geeking out leads to more gratitude and joy in life—and there is always room for more joy.

Animal Kingdom

Human beings are a part of the ecosystem of this planet, a vast web of connection. Unlike other animals, we have a distinctive type of consciousness that allows us to use language, invent, create, and understand beyond the scope of the rest of the animal kingdom. Some people might think that this justifies our treatment of habitats, environment, and other animals. But I feel that it calls for a different kind of role than we currently have, and a better relationship with the rest of the animal species on this planet. People elsewhere in the world, such as in Africa, have already taken on this role, but in the West, we still have a disconnected relationship with the environment and the animal kingdom, particularly when the majority of human beings live in cities.

In cities, the closest encounters we have with other animals are birds, rats and mice, squirrels, hedgehogs, foxes, raccoons (not in the UK), insects, and animals we keep as pets or companions. In the countryside, the range broadens to include creatures kept for farming, badgers, moles, and a wider range of amphibians. Most of us think of foxes and similar creatures as pests, because of the diseases they might carry, their behaviour when confronted with vulnerable humans, and their opportunism, such as knocking over bins and foraging amongst human waste. Our fear of some of these animals comes from a lack of understanding about the symbiotic relationship within the ecosystem, and because when we live in urban environments, we are more likely to live in close quarters with species that feed from our way of life—that have found ways to survive within the urban environment. We are, basically, afraid of being attacked or of contamination.

Another way that we come face to face with other animals is at the zoo, or the circus. When I was a child, my favourite places to visit were London Zoo and Woburn Safari Park. As an adult, I feel a great deal of discomfort at visiting the zoo, no matter how irresistible it is to see such a beautiful range of animals in close quarters. No matter how good the enclosures or how well looked after, these are still caged animals. There are two arguments for and against the nature of zoo husbandry in the twenty-first century. The first is conservation and education. The second is the number of 'excess' animals culled, the zoos that mistreat their animals, the number of zoo keeper deaths, and the fact that conservation is basically another word for breeding animals for captivity. Naively, I used to think that conservation meant that animals would be bred and then set free in the wild, but the different conditions of growing up in captivity contrasted with not growing up in their natural habitat means that they are not equipped with the skills necessary for survival. Usually, animals that have been used in zoos, circuses, and for other dubious and cruel entertainment or 'medical' purposes can be released into animal sanctuaries where they have appropriate care and an environment suitable for them. One such sanctuary is the Animals Asia Foundation's bear sanctuary, rehabilitating and caring for Asiatic black bears, cruelly used in Chinese bear farms and milked for their bile, which is used in Chinese medicine, despite having no real medical benefits.

Conservation is an important part of our role as human beings, and reflects our responsibility for the environment. Especially considering the ways in which we humans have damaged the ecosystem and built upon the environments these animals live in.

Poaching and trade have driven some animals towards the brink of extinction, and even extinct altogether. Human beings, in this respect, have failed in our duty to be caring, considerate and sustainable creatures. Our hunger for power, wealth, and even health means that we have viewed other animals as bounty to be bought and sold. In a culture that values animal rights, and the positive relationship we have with pets and companions, even with our focus on the welfare of animals, we are still not doing a good enough job of asking difficult questions and using our creativity to come up with solutions (other than zoos) for conservation. Protected land and conservation parks are a good start, but there is simply not enough support or protection against poachers. The people protecting these animals risk their lives every day so that these animals will be around for future generations. There are people doing good work with legitimate sanctuaries that need our support, whether through funding, volunteering, or publicity.

Some of the difficulty comes from how we see ourselves as being at top of the food chain, separate from and therefore more important than the rest of the animals we share the planet with. The reality is that we are not necessarily separate from them. We do erect walls, buildings, and cities to physically shelter us, using the planet's resources to do so, and yet so do other animals, using the world around them to create burrows, nests, dams, colonies, warrens, and hives. Surviving, and thriving, is important to all creatures on this planet, including us. Our ways of surviving and living are different to other species, but we have taken inspiration from nature for centuries, as well as using materials such as brick, sand, stone, wood, water, and plaster, amongst many other types of material, sourced from the earth. The building blocks of our lives, at least the parts not man-made, come from what we can shape with our hands, or outsource to other people and their machines. Microsystems, minuscule creatures creating a whole world we can barely see, exist with much the same behaviours as us—such as ants, with their workers and leaf-cutters, and intricate buildings.

Effectively, what our years of burning fossil fuels, factory pollution, and industrial-scale farming and trade systems have done to this planet is more visible and easy to see than ever before. Climate change isn't a myth or a contested belief. It's a real, tangible truth, measured by how the sea-level has risen, how the ice-caps are melting, polar-bears stranded alone in the middle of rapidly disappearing ground. Flooding has become a more common-place and devastating occurrence, all around the world. Weather systems change and upset the rest of the ecosystem—more droughts and lack of food, felling of forests, and wildfires, are slowly (and sometimes quickly) killing majestic animals that we may never see again. This is why countries are coming together and making commitments to reduce and eliminate their use of dirty fuels, to try and limit the damage we have already caused the planet. The good news is that climate change has been recognised as something we all have a responsibility to reduce, that waste and pollution are something it is possible to change, or at least curb. Still, complacency is not an option—if we look at how some countries are refusing to take responsibility for their part in reducing climate change, such as the US recently bowing out of the Paris Climate Agreement, and the UK government pushing through shale gas fracking, citizens need to put more pressure on policy-makers.

In the middle of all this, we also need to look at the corporations we buy products and services from, who are funding our governments, and provide all manner of products, services, and funding within society. These corporations often refuse to take responsibility for their destruction of habitats and indigenous communities. In the Borneo, for example, the destruction of rainforest has led to the near extinction of Orang-utans, gentle, intelligent creatures that depend on the forest for food and shelter. The palm-oil we find in many of our products comes from logging and destruction of their habitat, to make fields of palms. Palm-oil itself is not a particularly good oil for human beings, but it is cheap, therefore why it is in so many of our food products. Fortunately, the campaigns to raise awareness of these practices and to lobby the corporations responsible has had some measure of success. Still, as a result of the logging, humans have once again intervened; you are more likely to find Orang-utans in shelters and sanctuaries, many of them traumatised after being separated from their mothers and families. Our empathy has to extend both towards our fellow human beings and the rest of the animal kingdom if we are going to make this planet a better place to live.

My childhood visits to the zoo inspired a lifelong love of animals. I collected a series of fact-files, *The Wildlife Factfile*, and watched as many wildlife documentaries as I possibly could. David Attenborough's *Trials of Life* was the first programme I watched that gave me some measure of understanding of how delicate and diverse the animal kingdom is. Everything in the ecosystem is connected—from the weather, to the flora and fauna, to the air quality, the richness and variety of insects, to the mammals. If you agree that we are part of the mammal family, with our warm blood (and even if you don't), then we are also a part of that connected web. It has only been the last twenty years when I have come to understand this more deeply and how we must step up to be stewards of this kingdom. It starts, as always, with the willingness to develop your sense of wonder and to educate yourself the best you can, to observe with an open mind. Even if you find many aspects of the animal kingdom slightly disgusting (I know I do!), that is just a part of the strangeness of life. Nature is strange, wild, ugly, beautiful, messy, and ordered, all at the same time.

To make lasting change we need to take real interest in the schemes and research taking place around environment and wildlife. Complacency is no longer an option, and the people who have been on the front lines of animal and environment protection have understood this. As with anything else, taking interest in, and educating yourself about the world around us takes time, and patience, but ultimately, it's worthwhile, if we are going to try to make the future—and the present—a better place for all the creatures, humans included, on this planet. It's difficult to know what to do when governments and world leaders are more concerned with turning a profit than safeguarding the planet for future generations. But there is always hope in the people who do try to make a difference, and it is those people we need to find ways to support—by spreading information, by actively doing what you feel will make a difference, no matter how small, and by doing your best to ensure the survival of other animals—planting wildflowers for bees, adopting cats or dogs rather than buying from pet shops (or breeders), and perhaps considering having a few days a week (even one day) where you eat vegetarian or vegan food (or even become completely vegan). Cultivating greater empathy for creatures that populate our world even if you find them creepy or unhygienic. They have every right to exist on this planet too. I don't think anyone has all the answers, but greater awareness of how to make our planet better is always a good place to start.

On Staying Soft

*'Be soft. Do not let the world make you hard. Do not
let the pain make you hate. Do not let the bitterness
steal your sweetness. Take pride that even though the
rest of the world may disagree, you still believe it to be
a beautiful place.'*

—Iain Thomas, *I Wrote This For You.*

It is easy, with the amount of bad news we receive on a daily basis,
to turn away and give in to fear and cynicism. I don't know
everything about the ins and outs of politics. Both UK, USA,
and international politics can be confusing, with their archaic,
tangled laws and constantly changing agendas. It's easy to look away
and get on with our lives, scoffing at politicians, believing that
nothing will change if we use our voices, believing that the easiest
fix is to close our hearts and let other people worry about themselves.
There are so many different issues demanding our attention,
disasters and wars across the world, human right abuses, people
fighting for equality, trying to defend the rights that took so long to
achieve, which are always under threat. The environment, some
animals close to extinction, housing crises, homelessness, a global
tilt towards far-right thinking.

You'd be forgiven for wanting to give up, and let other people deal with it. You might feel that all this pain is too much, or that some people deserve your hate and bitterness. That you may as well stop reading the headlines and taking notice of what is happening in your country and in the world because it's all going to come crashing down anyway. Leave the politicians and the corporations, and the drama and the fear, and the desperation and pain to fester away from your life. No matter that everything politicians do has an effect—whether immediate or in the future—on what happens in your life. It's easier to stop educating yourself rather than constantly reaching for enlightenment. To simply switch it all off and stay away from anything that could disrupt your equilibrium.

The truth is that I've come close to doing exactly this. It's healthy to have breaks, to give yourself time away. As wonderful as it is to be living, breathing, feeling, and empathising creatures, there comes a point when too much information, pain, and negativity can wear you down. It makes you feel hopeless, like there is nothing you can do. That all the changes people suggest you make to generate change would take too much time and energy away from your own life. It's true that you can't do it all. You can't possibly rush around like a whirling dervish signing lots of petitions, going on a march a week, and constantly raising money for causes that matter to you. You can support the efforts of other people—share their fundraising, educate yourself on an issue so that the next time it comes up in conversation you can inform other people. You can be selective and sign the petitions that seem the most promising and necessary to you in that moment in time. And you could choose to be a part of a collective of specialised issues within a movement—each of us working on our little piece of the jigsaw, each win a small step forward.

The trick of it all is to learn to filter. Some days it will be exhausting to do any kind of activism or have intense conversations with other people. You might find yourself going around and round with the same old arguments and debates. As a rule, I avoid debating online now—debates are often prone to becoming overheated and hostile, when someone misunderstands something, or feels a certain tone is being used. I make the effort to listen to other voices, to take in articles from a variety of sources, blogs, and communities, to try not to fall into the trap of assuming my own view is the correct view. I am constantly building on my own education. There are as many perspectives as there are people. Of course, free speech is also an important, necessary thing. It doesn't mean that someone gets to abuse someone, to attack someone personally or abuse them, but that they are entitled to their point of view even if you don't agree with it. There is a difference between a point of view and hate speech and prejudice. That distinction is one that people conveniently forget when taking part in online (and, increasingly, offline) debates.

Matt Haig, in his book *Notes On A Nervous Planet*, writes about how the world has become more frantic, louder, with more information at our fingertips than ever before. It isn't as easy to 'switch off' the news as it used to be. Our smartphones are an ever-present presence in our lives. They hold the promise of limitless information and distraction. We are more anxious, more stressed, and getting less sleep than we used to. The boundaries we used to have between the images and information sent our way through the TV or the newspaper and our mental wellbeing has been filed down, and it is easier to be afraid of the unknown—or increasingly, the 'known'. What do we do when faced with an ever-present stream of information? We have to learn what we want in our lives. There is a fine line between being informed and being overwhelmed. Boundaries matter more than ever—time with our phones switched off, time spent with the people around us, or reading a book or watching a film—or interacting with the tangible, real world around you.

Another trick is to seek out the kind of news and statistics that show what progress we are making. There is such a thing as happy news—the kind of news that shows people rebuilding their lives after disaster, a family reuniting after being forced to migrate from their war-torn country—myriad everyday events that are beautiful and worth knowing. For example, Emily Coxhead's *The Happy Newspaper*, highlighting news from all over the world that restores our faith in humanity. At the end of 2016, through all the sadness and difficulty, I read a host of articles detailing the good that had happened, the progress made for human rights, the environment, and for animals saved from the brink of extinction. We need this knowledge too, to save us from despair. The greatest issue with modern news reporting is that bad news sells more papers, and therefore we are more likely to infer that the world is a dangerous, cynical, and wildly scary place. This puts more psychological and emotional strain on people, creating extra stress and anxiety— therefore making us more likely to act (or not act) out of fear, and more likely to be distrustful and feel more hatred.

Most newspapers are owned by corporations that have a vested interest in pushing a particular agenda, slanting the news and opinion pieces towards subtle or overt political interests. What is more important here is not what your political leanings are, but how we can begin to think for ourselves, to try and take the qualities of kindness and intelligent empathy out into the world with us. We live in a time that appears more politically polarised, in which we have largely forgotten what it means to create dialogue and understanding; to listen to each other. No bridges can be crossed without learning how to listen: listening may not mean accepting someone's point of view, but it does mean trying, as far as possible, to understand why that person thinks or feels that way. Again, this doesn't mean accepting hatred—no racism, misogyny, ableism, homophobia, or transphobia is acceptable—but it does mean creating a dialogue, opening minds, and keeping a channel open for education.

Only you can judge just how much of something is worth your time or energy. Activism begins with educating yourself, always: it begins with reading and thinking, talking (online or in person) with other people, slowly building up confidence in your knowledge of a subject. It begins with making space for listening, particularly if you're a member of a privileged group in society—white, middle/upper class, high education, male, heterosexual or able bodied—and for being patient. It's impossible to know everything about an issue—which is why we need to own up to our mistakes, learn from them, and try again. There is a very real fear that we might say or do something wrong, but at least we are aware of that possibility and the worst that can happen is that we will know not to do or say it again, and why it is wrong. I've made plenty of mistakes and held a number of opinions that have been tested and adapted, dropped, and changed. Staying open to that means we are doing life right; being open minded and seeing that not all the assumptions and ideas we hold are the only ones, or the 'correct' ones.

Why is softness more important than ever? It has an important part to play in acknowledging each other's humanity and capacity for understanding. To close ourselves off, even in a time of uncertainty and overwhelm, is closing ourselves off to one of the most important aspects of human nature—connection. No matter who we are or how we see the world, to connect with others is an intrinsic part of experiencing life. Without it, we become small, only concerned with our own lives, wrapped up in problems and fear. To be soft is to be curious and interested in other people—to give them attention and understand both yourself and the world a little better. Our identities are shaped both by internal experience and external contact with other individuals. We only truly find more meaning by discovering what we have to give to the world—through all kinds of ways, from volunteering, teaching, writing articles and blog posts, activism, community, and collaborating, amongst the many other ways there are to give something of ourselves and gain something back. Keeping that channel open is the epitome of allowing ourselves to be open to change, and to changing the world—in whatever ways we can—through big actions or small.

In my case, what I can give is my constantly evolving knowledge and understanding, and the expression of that through creativity and words. It matters to me when something I've written makes a difference to someone—even just one person—and it matters to me that I create a dialogue between my writing and the people reading it. Whether or not they begin that dialogue with me or with other people doesn't matter—what matters is that something is sparked. This is the gift of creativity—not to hoard it for yourself, but to send it out into the world, and see it snowball into more creativity and ideas. I'm understanding that activism is an expanding concept in the world we live in now—it can be in-person activism but I'm a believer that ideas—both good and bad—have the capacity to change the world. Many books, poems, and articles I've read are testament to how an idea can change your perspective, can enlarge it. Words are powerful, and even in this world of 'fake news' and 'alternative facts', we can learn to think for ourselves and see the world with an open mind.

Outro: Fitting The Jigsaw

All of us are a culmination of many different circumstances—from our upbringing and childhood, to the choices we make and the barriers we experience as adults. The times we live in now are noisy, and confusing, often stressful, and add extra pressures difficult to carry. With this book, I wanted to show that there are different ways to think about life. That maybe we don't need to be so hard on ourselves. That we can opt-out in the ways that work for us and make lives that are more in line with our values. That it's possible to help each other to thrive.

What matters the most is that we find and keep close the people that we best connect with. That we continue to learn from life and the wisdom of others—whether found in a book or from late-night conversations. Continuing to learn throughout our lives is something that makes this messy, imperfect, and sometimes difficult existence worth it. You can learn how to look after yourself better, and how to love others better. How to be your own champion, and how to champion the efforts of others.

In this book, I've written as much as I can about what I know, and what I've experienced, and what I feel. I don't know how much of it will be of use to you, reading this now. I hope it is useful, that reading this has given you solace, has helped you to understand yourself a bit better. I wrote this book over the course of two and a half years—two of them some of the hardest I have experienced, when I was going through a number of painful experiences, and writing these essays gave me purpose when life seemed uncertain. Coming through those two years, I've learnt a lot more about myself and the people around me, about life itself, and what is most important. Even so, I know that life has a lot more to teach me. Writing has much more to teach me too.

We are always changing, always opening up and moving. We don't grow from the ground—we're not plants. We grow by experiencing, by seeing, by doing. We grow by listening and being patient. Our preferences and what we enjoy change over time. Everything we have done up to this point has given us an education, whether those experiences were good or bad. I've lost people, places, cats, communities and yet, I don't regret any of it. Sometimes, I grieve, but I don't regret. And neither should you—be all that you are, and try to let go of the hurts. You are who you are now, with the choices you make going forward from this moment in time.

I hope you take the time to celebrate your body and everything it can do. None of us has a body that can do everything—or that will always be able to do what it can now. You don't have to love your body, or believe that it's amazing, but I hope you can at least learn to like it, accept it, and appreciate what it does. Part of that is also accepting that people come in many different shapes and sizes and that we have no right to pass comment on other people's bodies. Learn to respect your own body, and respect the bodies of other people too. It's good, too, to sometimes laugh at the strangeness of human bodies—that sometimes you might sweat on the tube in the middle of winter.

If you have your tribe, the people who you can talk to about anything, love them well. If you don't yet, that's okay too. Love is action: do love, show it in respectful, kind ways. It took me a while to find my people. Some of them have been there for years—my sister, my husband, old friends—but others have come into my life when it was just right. It happened after the loss of a community that

I believed was my tribe at the time. Afterwards, picking up all the pieces, I discovered that the people who care stick around. That maybe, after all, losing something means you also find something.

Life is this magnificent adventure, no matter whether we travel widely or never leave the country we're born in. The smallest joy can imbue it with meaning. You don't have to do big, exciting, noticeable things to make a difference to other people, to the planet. Supporting campaigns doesn't mean you always have to go on marches or give up your job to go and live in a commune.

Taking part in activism can happen every day with the choices you make—recycling, volunteering, adopting animals, writing emails to your MP, donating money to a campaign or supporting small businesses. Some effort is required to learn more about our impact on the planet and about different campaigns—perhaps by reading as widely as you can and learning to listen better—but it's something that is worth that effort. I believe in lifelong self-education, in following your interests and being curious, just for the sake of it. It makes for interesting conversations, and more importantly, a joyful life.

What you hold in your hand here is a certain perspective on life, a collection of ideas, some better than others, some food for thought, that just happened to want to take the form of essays: they don't cover everything, but offer fragments, pieces of a jigsaw that don't always fit together, but form parts of a whole. In the end, that is what we are—fragments—pieces that come together in a jumble of experiences, thoughts, values, and traits.

Acknowledgements

To Daniel, Beverley and Pete, Sarah and Matt, thank you for your love and encouragement, without which this book wouldn't have been written. To my friends, you know who you are—who have been waiting for this book for years—thank you for your enthusiasm and patience. To the many people I've met over the years who have told me their stories and given me the desire to tell my own. And to the readers of my blog, my blog friends around the world, and the wonderful communities of people I have come across, thank you for showing me what is possible.

Notes

Citations and Book Recommendations

Part One: Living in a Body

Body Positive

1. Aphramor, L. and Bacon, L. (2014) *Body Respect: What Conventional Health Books Get Wrong, Leave Out, and Just Plain Fail To Understand About Weight.* Dallas, TX, BenBella Books.
2. Bacon, L. (2010) *Health At Every Size: The Surprising Truth About Your Weight.* Dallas, TX, BenBellas Books.
3. Baker, Jes (2018) *Landwhale: Why Insults Are Just Really Cute Nicknames, Body Image Is Hard, and Diets Can Kiss My Ass.* Berkeley, CA, Seal Press.
4. Crabbe, Meghan Jane (2017) *Body Positive Power.* Vermilion.
5. Wolf, Naomi (1991) *The Beauty Myth.* New York, Vintage.

On Health and Radical Body Positivity

1. Aphramor, L. and Bacon, L. (2014) *Body Respect: What Conventional Health Books Get Wrong, Leave Out, and Just Plain Fail To Understand About Weight.* Dallas, TX, BenBella Books.

Fatshion and Taking Up Space

1. Baker, J (2015) *Things No One Will Tell Fat Girls: A Handbook Of Unapologetic Living*. Berkeley, CA, Seal Press.
2. Tea, M (2007) *It's So You: 35 Women Write About Personal Expression Through Fashion and Style*. Berkeley, CA, Seal Press.
3. Tovar, V. (2012) *Hot and Heavy: Fierce Fat Girls On Love, Life and Fashion*. Seattle, WA, Seal Press.

Living As Woman

1. Bates, L (2015) *Everyday Sexism*. UK, Simon and Schuster.
2. Gay, R (2014) *Bad Feminist: Essays*. London, Corsair.
3. Ngozi Adichie, C (2014) *We Should All Be Feminists*. London, Fourth Estate.
4. Penny, L (2018) *Bitch Doctrine: Essays For Dissenting Adults*. London, Bloomsbury.
5. Solnit, R (2014) *Men Explain Things To Me*. London, Granta.

Brain Music

1. *Lost and Sound*. (2012). [DVD] Directed by L. Dryden. UK: Animal Monday and Little By Little.
2. Coleman, N (2013) *The Train In The Night: A Story Of Music and Loss*. London, Vintage.

Part Two: Matters of the Heart

An Ode To Love

1. Appignanesi, L (2012) *All About Love: Anatomy of an Unruly Emotion*. London, Virago.

2. Hooks, b (2001) *All About Love: New Visions.* New York, William Morrow.

Hygge and the Little Things

1. Balslev, L (2018) *The Little Book of Fika: The Uplifting Daily Ritual of the Swedish Coffee Break.* Kansas City, Andrew McMeel Publishing.
2. Brones, A (2017) *Live Lagom: Balanced Living, The Swedish Way.* London, Ebury Press.
3. Garcia, G. and Miralles, F. (2017) *Ikigai: The Japanese Secret to a Long and Happy Life.* London, Penguin.
4. Wiking, Meik (2016) *The Little Book of Hygge: The Danish Way To Live Well.* London, Penguin Life.
5. Wiking, Meik (2018) *The Little Book of Lykke: The Danish Search for the World's Happiest People.* London, Penguin.

Loneliness

1. Atwood, M (1981) 'Spelling' in *True Stories.* New York, Simon and Schuster.
2. Laing, O (2017) *The Lonely City.* Edinburgh, Canongate.
3. Maitland, S (2010) *A Book of Silence.* London, Granta.
4. Sarton, M (1992) *Journal of a Solitude.* New York, W.W. Norton and Company.

The Imaginative Leap of Empathy

1. Bloom, P (2014) '*Against Empathy*' published in The Boston Review, September 10th 2014.
2. Bloom, P (2018) *Against Empathy: The Case for Rational Compassion.* London, Vintage.

3. Krznaric, R (2013) *The Wonderbox: Curious Histories of How to Live.* London, Profile.

4. Krznaric, R (2014) *Empathy: A Handbook For Revolution.* London, Rider Books.

Why Jane? A Truth Universally Acknowledged

1. Penny, L (2018) *Bitch Doctrine: Essays For Dissenting Adults.* London, Bloomsbury.

2. Tomalin, C (2012) *Jane Austen: A Life.* London, Penguin.

3. Worsley, L (2018) *Jane Austen At Home: A Biography.* London, Hodder and Stoughton.

Heal

1. Avis, R (2018) *Dinosaur Hearted.* Long Beach, CA, Hostile 17 Print.

2. Haig, M (2015) *Reasons To Stay Alive.* Edinburgh, Canongate.

3. Haig, M (2018) *Notes On A Nervous Planet.* Edinburgh, Canongate.

4. Koren, L (2008) *Wabi-Sabi: For Artists, Designers, Poets and Philosophers.* Point Reyes, CA, Imperfect Publishing.

5. Lewis, G (2006) *Sunbathing In The Rain: A Cheerful Book About Depression.* London, Harper Perennial.

Part Three: Thinking and Dreaming

On Introversion

1. Cain, S (2013) *Quiet: The Power of Introverts In A World That Can't Stop Talking.* London, Penguin.

2. Chung, M (2016) *The Irresistible Introvert: Harness The Power of Quiet Charisma in a Loud World.* New York, Skyhorse.

3. Granneman, J (2017) *The Secret Lives of Introverts: Inside Our Hidden World*. New York, Skyhorse.

4. Helgoe, L (2013) *Introvert Power: Why Your Inner Life Is Your Hidden Strength*. Naperville, Ill, Sourcebooks.

The Search For Meaning and Purpose

1. Brown, B (2013) *Daring Greatly: How The Courage To Be Vulnerable Transforms The Way We Live, Love, Parent and Lead*. London, Portfolio Penguin.

2. Brown, B (2010) *The Gifts of Imperfection*. Center City, Minnesota, Hazelden.

3. Esfahani Smith, E (2018) *The Power of Meaning: The True Route to Happiness*. London, Penguin Random House.

Indolence: The Pleasure of Doing Nothing

1. Soojung-Kim Pang, A (2018) *Rest: Why You Get More Done When You Work Less*. London, Penguin Life.

2. Sunim, H (2018) *The Things You Can See Only When You Slow Down: How To Be Calm In A Busy World*. London, Penguin Life.

3. Walker, M (2018) *Why We Sleep: The New Science of Sleep and Dreams*. London, Penguin.

On Fear

1. Cotton, F (2017) *Calm: Working Through Life's Daily Stresses To Find a Peaceful Centre*. London, Orion Spring.

2. Goldberg, N (2005) *Writing Down The Bones*. Boston, Massachusetts, Shambhala.

3. Haig, M (2018) *Notes On A Nervous Planet*. Edinburgh, Canongate.

4. Rayner, S (2017) *Making Friends With Anxiety*. Brighton, Creative Pumpkin Publishing.

5. Wax, R (2014) *Sane New World: Taming The Mind*. London, Hodder and Stoughton.

Surfacing

1. Haig, M (2015) *Reasons To Stay Alive*. Edinburgh, Canongate.

2. Hardy, J (2017) *The Self Care Project: How To Let Go Of Frazzle and Make Time For You*. London, Orion Spring.

3. Lewis, G (2006) *Sunbathing In The Rain: A Cheerful Book About Depression*. London, Harper Perennial.

4. Noakes, M (2017) *The Little Book Of Self Care*. London, Ebury Press.

The Real Meaning Of Inclusion

1. Davis, L. J (2016) *The Disability Studies Reader*. New York, Routledge.

2. Oliva, G (2004) *Alone In The Mainstream: A Deaf Woman Remembers Public School*. Washington, Gallaudet University Press.

3. Shakespeare, T (2018) *Disability: The Basics*. New York, Routledge.

Highly Sensitive People

1. Aron, E. N (1999) The Highly Sensitive Person: How To Thrive When The World Overwhelms You. London, Harper Thorsons.

2. Sand, I (2016) *Highly Sensitive People In An Insensitive World*. London, Jessica Kingsley.

Part Four: Writing and Creating

Why Write?

1. Cohen, S (2016) *Fierce On The Page: Become The Writer You Were Meant To Be And Succeed On Your Own Terms.* Ohio, Writer's Digest Books.
2. Cron, L (2016) *Story Genius.* New York, Ten Speed Press.
3. Goldberg, N (2005) *Writing Down The Bones.* Boston, Massachusetts, Shambhala.
4. King, S (2012) *On Writing: A Memoir of the Craft.* London, Hodder.
5. Shapiro, D (2013) *Still Writing: The Pleasures and Perils Of a Creative Life.* New York, Atlantic Monthly Press.
6. Wendig, C (2013) *The Kick-Ass Writer: 1001 Ways To Write Great Fiction, Get Published, and Earn Your Audience.* Ohio, Writer's Digest Books.

Choosing Encouragement

1. Anske, K (2013) *Blue Sparrow: Tweets on Writing, Reading, and Other Creative Nonsense.* Seattle, Ksenia Anske.
2. Herron, R (2018) *Onward, Writer!: 29 Encouraging Letters To Your Inner Writer.* HGA Publishing.
3. Shapiro, D (2013) *Still Writing: The Pleasures and Perils Of a Creative Life.* New York, Atlantic Monthly Press.
4. Wendig, C (2017) *Damn Fine Story: Mastering The Tools and Architecture of a Powerful Narrative.* Ohio, Writer's Digest Books.

Energy

1. Csikszentmihalyi, M (2002) *Flow: The Psychology of Happiness*. London, Rider.

2. Burstein, J, and Andersen, K (2012) *Spark: How Creativity Works*. New York, Harper.

3. Kaufman, S.B, and Gregoire, C (2016) *Wired To Create: Discover The 10 Things Great Artists, Writers and Innovators Do Differently*. London, Vermilion.

4. Wolff, J (2010) *Focus: Use The Power Of Targeted Thinking To Get More Done*. UK, Pearson Business.

Poetry Resurgence

1. Avis, R (2016) *Sack Nasty: Prison Poetry*. Long Beach, CA, Hostile 17 Print.

2. Duffy, C. A (1999) *The World's Wife*. London, Picador.

3. Duffy, C. A (2002) *Feminine Gospels*. London, Picador.

4. Gill, N (2016) *Your Soul Is A River*. Thought Catalogue.

5. Kaur, R (2015) *Milk and Honey*. Kansas City, Andrew McMeel Publishing.

6. Kaur, R (2017) *The Sun and Her Flowers*. London, Simon and Schuster.

7. Oliver, M (1994) *Dream Work*. New York, Atlantic Monthly Press.

8. Waheed, N (2014) *Nejma*. Createspace.

Part Five: Society and Identity

Sound Memories

1. Cohen, L. H. (1994) *Train Go Sorry: Inside a Deaf World*. New York: Vintage, Random House.

2. Cyrus, B., Katz, E. and Cheyney, C., and Parsons, F. M. (2005) *Deaf Women's Lives: Three Self Portraits.* Washington: Gallaudet University Press.

3. Heppner, C. M. (1992) *Seeds of Disquiet.* Washington: Gallaudet University Press.

4. Laborit, E. (1998) *The Cry of the Gull.* Washington: Gallaudet University Press.

5. Oliva, G. A. (2004) *Alone in the Mainstream: A Deaf Woman Remembers Public School.* Washington: Gallaudet University Press.

Girl, Woman, Feminine, Feminist

1. Ahmed, S (2017) *Living A Feminist Life.* Durham and London, Duke University Press.

2. Cixous, H. (1976) *The Laugh of the Medusa.* Translated by Keith Cohen and Paula Cohen. Signs: Journal of Women in Culture and Society 1(4): 875-893.

3. Laborit, E. (1998) *The Cry of the Gull.* Washington: Gallaudet University Press.

4. Moran, C (2012) *How To Be A Woman.* London, Ebury Press.

5. Solnit, R (2017) *The Mother Of All Questions: Further Feminisms.* London, Granta.

How To Be A Geek

1. Hurley, K (2016) *The Geek Feminist Revolution.* New York, TOR.

2. Segal, S. H. (2011) *Geek Wisdom: The Sacred Teachings Of Nerd Culture.* Philadelphia, PA, Quirk.

Animal Kingdom

1. De Waal, F (2017) *Are We Smart Enough To Know How Smart Animals Are?* London, Granta.
2. Foster, C (2016) *Being A Beast.* London, Profile Books.
3. Laing, O (2013) *Gossip From The Forest: The Tangled Roots Of Our Forests and Fairytales.* London, Granta.
4. Moss, S (2017) *Wild Kingdom: Bringing Back Britain's Wildlife.* London, Vintage.
5. Wohlleben, P (2018) *The Inner Life Of Animals: Surprising Observations of a Hidden World.* London, Vintage.

On Staying Soft

1. Solnit, R (2016) *Hope In The Dark: Untold Histories, Wild Possibilities.* Edinburgh, Canongate.
2. Thomas, I (2011) *I Wrote This For You.* Central Avenue Publishing.

About The Author

Elizabeth is a deaf writer, activist, and feminist who lives in London with her husband, Daniel, and their cat, Coco, short for Chocolat. She has been a blogger for thirteen years, and an arts and culture journalist since 2011. She has two degrees, a BA in Sociology, and an MA in  Women's Studies, both from The University of York. A self-described bookish geek, foodie, and film fan, she loves nothing more than curling up on the sofa with a cup of tea, book or film and a cat or two for company.

Printed in Great Britain
by Amazon

37833150R00154